GEO KNITS

10 LESSONS AND PROJECTS FOR KNITTING STRIPES, CHEVRONS, TRIANGLES, POLKA DOTS, AND MORE

LARK
New York

An Imprint of Sterling Publishing Co., Inc.
1166 Avenue of the Americas
New York, NY 10036

ISBN: 978-1-4547-1013-4

33614057754805

Distributed by Sterling Publishing Co., Inc.
c/o Canadian Manda Group,
664 Annette Street,
Toronto, Ontario, Canada M6S 2C8

For information about custom editions, special sales,
and premium and coporate purchases, please contact
Sterling Sales at 800-805-5489 or specialsales@
sterlingpublishing.com.

Manufactured in China

10 9 8 7 6 5 4 3 2 1

sterlingpublishing.com
larkcrafts.com

Photography by Simon Pask

GEO KNITS

10 LESSONS AND PROJECTS FOR KNITTING STRIPES, CHEVRONS, TRIANGLES, POLKA DOTS, AND MORE

MARY JANE MUCKLESTONE

LARK
New York

CONTENTS

6

Introduction

8

How to Use This Book

20

Lesson 1: Garter Stitch Stripes

36

Lesson 3: Diagonal Colorwork Stripes

10

Get Some Geo Inspo!

44

Lesson 4: Garter Stitch Triangles

28

Lesson 2: Stockinette Stitch Stripes

18

CHAPTER 1: The Lessons

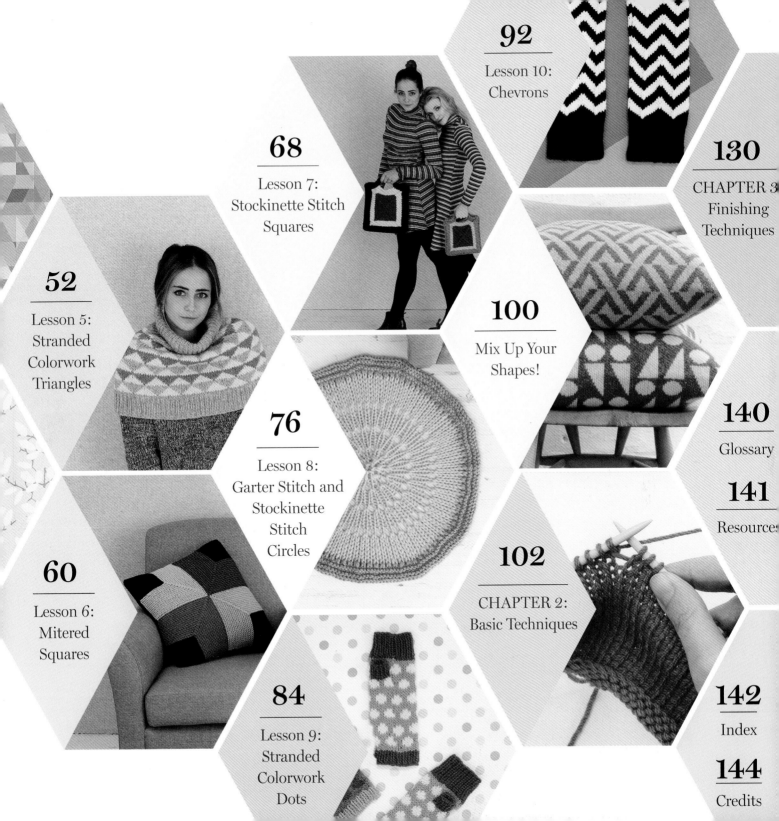

92

Lesson 10: Chevrons

130

CHAPTER 3
Finishing Techniques

68

Lesson 7: Stockinette Stitch Squares

52

Lesson 5: Stranded Colorwork Triangles

100

Mix Up Your Shapes!

140

Glossary

141

Resources

76

Lesson 8: Garter Stitch and Stockinette Stitch Circles

60

Lesson 6: Mitered Squares

102

CHAPTER 2: Basic Techniques

142

Index

144

Credits

84

Lesson 9: Stranded Colorwork Dots

INTRODUCTION

Geometric shapes and patterns are the foundations of the design world. Ever-popular in fashion, home goods, and architecture, and found in nature, math, and science, they're a truly fundamental part of all design. Geometric shapes, prints, and structures have an enduring freshness. They are patterns that continue to evolve and always look contemporary.

Simply by learning to knit some basic geometric shapes, we're able to create striking pieces without the need for advanced skills. Knitting should be about creating something you love, without it driving you crazy in the process! Geo knits are the perfect way to do just that.

In this book, I have included some of the most important, yet basic, knitting techniques. You will learn new skills through the process of creating modern knits from bold shapes. Once you have these skills, not only will you be able to put them together to make other, unique designs, but you will have a better understanding of knitting as a whole. Everything in this book has been designed to teach you something new, and

increase your knowledge of knitting in an easy and understandable way. Knit through this book and by the end, you should be confident enough to figure out and tackle more advanced designs. I have included lots of inspiration along the way to keep you going—knitting is all about learning new things so that fear and anxiety is removed from the experience. You do have the ability to create your dream item yourself! Looking to the catwalk, or online knitting sites and seeing how shapes and stitches are combined is the perfect way for you to expand your knowledge and maybe even design knits of your own too.

Take time to look through the Basic Techniques section at the

back of this book and make sure you're comfortable with all the techniques we use, and then begin the lessons. The chapters flow from shape to shape and start with the easiest stitches in each section first. Once you have mastered these, you can also check out the Mix Up Your Shapes! pages, which include lots of ideas on how to combine the shapes and techniques that you have learnt. Feel free to adapt, add colors, or plan new designs as you go! The important thing is to practice and experiment. Don't be afraid to make mistakes and don't chide yourself if things don't go exactly to plan. Knitting should be fun and the good thing is, that you can only get better.

HOW TO USE THIS BOOK

Unlock the mystery behind garter stitch stripes vs stockinette stitch stripes, try super simple stranded colorwork for geometric shapes within the fabric of your knitting, and use basic increases and decreases to build geometric shaped pieces which are the foundation of knitted garments and shawls. The 10 simple lessons in this book will take you through all the techniques you need in order to knit with bold geometric shapes. Each lesson includes a brief introduction to the technique, an inspiration board to set your needles aquiver, a simple lesson, and a beautiful project for you to create using your new knitting skills.

The lessons build on one another as you move through the book, so start at the beginning and work from lesson 1 to 10 for a full introduction to geometric knitting. However, if you are already confident in your knitting skills, or you really want to try a certain shape, you can jump in wherever.

Take a look at the mood boards for some geometric inspiration! Projects from knitwear designers are included throughout the book, see page 144 for details of where to find these patterns.

Charts and sketches will help you get your ideas down on paper.

Each new lesson starts with an introduction to what you will learn on the following pages.

LESSON ONE

GARTER STITCH STRIPES

Knit quick and easy **garter stitch** to create bold **stripe** patterns in contrasting colors.

Stripes create a linear look that will never go out of style. They are the "neutral" of the print world, pairing easily with other patterns. Horizontal, vertical, or diagonal stripes demand attention.

In knitting, stripes are a great introduction to working with multiple colors as they can be easily mixed and stacked into interesting patterns. Garter stitch is the perfect stitch to play with this effect. Often dismissed as a beginner stitch, the distinctive 3D stripe made by garter stitch ridges can be utilized in many creative ways.

This distinctive ridged stripe, and the fantastic thick, squishy fabric it creates, comes about because garter stitch uses only one stitch—the knit stitch. Every stitch on every row is knit. Two rows of knit stitch create a ridge, which is itself a textural stripe, and continuing in the same color creates a series of horizontal ridges. Unlike some other stitch patterns, stitches in garter stitch will look the same on the front and back.

However, when garter stitch stripes are made in color, there are interesting and surprising effects. When a new color is introduced to make different colored stripes, the two sides of the fabric will look different, making a broken ridge effect that can be used as a design element when creating striped knits, as for the Möbius Cowl on page 25.

Inspiration!

Rainbow Magicowl by Elizabeth Brassard

Olana Slouch by Grace Akhrem

Varying widths can drastically alter a look.

20

You will see how other designers incorporate the same shapes into their designs.

LESSON THREE

INTRODUCING STRANDED COLORWORK

To master stranded colorwork knitting, you'll need to learn to hold and work with two colors of yarn at the same time, alternating the colors used for the stitches. The yarn not in use is stranded across the back of the fabric—these are the floats. The best way to learn this is simply to practice—with time you will get the hang of it! You will also need to learn to read charts. Instead of colorwork instructions being written out in words, charts are given, providing a visual guide to the pattern.

FAIR ISLE KNITTING

Fair Isle knitting is a very specific regional style of stranded knitting that was developed on Fair Isle, one of the Scottish Shetland Islands. Traditional Fair Isle knitting is stranded knitting, worked in the round, with never more than two colors in a single row. It should be knit from yarn produced in Shetland, from the wool of the Shetland breed of sheep. It is a sophisticated style, which produces some of the most fantastic color effects, offering subtle shadings or a riot of color.

Fair Isle garments are often made up of horizontal bands, sporting larger and smaller motifs; border patterns and peerie patterns respectively. The pattern motifs themselves are usually geometric, with four or more lines of symmetry, making them easy to memorize. Motifs usually have no more than an inch, or about eight stitches, between color changes to avoid long floats.

READING CHARTS

Knitting charts are presented on a square grid or graph, where each square represents a single stitch. Every horizontal row of squares indicates a row of the pattern, which will be repeated the number of times required to circle your garment. Each chart usually represents an entire single pattern motif, which also will be repeated for the number of times required to complete your garment. When knitting circularly, read the chart from right to left, and bottom to top. Circular knitting charts are numbered up the right side, indicating the round number. Take a look at page 115 for in-depth instructions on how to read charts.

LEFT Diagonal lines can be arranged to make bold chevron patterns.

In this chart and the chart below, a single pattern motif or repeat is outlined in red and multiple repeats are shown in order to illustrate the appearance of the final knitted fabric.

LEFT Flip your pattern to create vertical zigzag lines.

38

Swatches, charts, or illustrations will help you practice your stitches and designs.

Need a bit more info? Check for these useful boxes.

BASIC TECHNIQUES

BASIC STITCHES

The most elemental techniques of all knitting are the knit stitch and the purl stitch. Essentially, purling is like backwards knitting. Once you have mastered knit and purl, you are halfway to making almost anything you would like!

KNIT STITCH

Hold the yarn and needles whichever way you prefer.

1 Insert the right-hand needle into the first stitch on the left-hand needle, from the left to the right.
2 Wrap the yarn under the tip and then over the right-hand needle and draw the yarn through the stitch.
3 Slip the stitch off the left-hand needle and onto the right-hand needle.

PURL STITCH

Hold the yarn and needles whatever way you prefer.

1 Bring the working yarn to the front.
2 Insert the right-hand needle into the first stitch on the left-hand needle, from right to left in the front.
3 Bring the yarn in front of the right-hand needle, wrap the yarn over the needle and draw the yarn through the stitch.
4 Slip the stitch off the left-hand needle and onto the right-hand needle.

118

Step-by-step photographs show clearly how to complete each skill.

Before beginning a project check out the techniques chapters, pages 102–139, for all the basic techniques and stitches used in the book.

GET SOME GEO INSPO!

Pages 10–15 are packed with inspiration from fashion archives, interior design, and modern knitwear trends. These mood boards reveal how versatile geometric shapes are and the many different ways in which they can be used to create bold and beautiful designs.

You can use the simple grids on pages 16–17 to jot down ideas, inspiration, and start sketching your geo designs. With your notepad bursting with future projects, you can then turn to the lessons and projects to start your geo journey.

STRIPES

Nautical, pinstripe, chunky, even, or random—stripes are truly everywhere! Don't discount them as plain. Using thin or fat stripes, monochrome colors or rainbow hues, a million effects can be achieved.

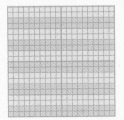

LEFT Turn to page 16 and use the graph paper to sketch out some of your own ideas for designs using striking stripes.

Get creative! Make horizontal knitted stripes vertical by turning the piece on end.

Random Stripes by Grace Akhrem

Garter stitch creates a thick textured stripe while stockinette stitch is smooth and flat.

Turntable by Hilary Smith Callis

By staggering the pattern stitches you can create diagonal stripes in stranded knitting. See page 40 for an eye-catching tablet case.

11

TRIANGLES

A useful trick to understand the potential of triangular shapes is to draw them in black and white and notice the negative and positive areas in a design. Observe how placing a triangle in a different orientation can completely change the effect it has, and how triangles of different sizes can be used in a single pattern repeat.

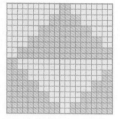

LEFT By drawing on graph paper (see page 16) you can begin to experiment with different patterns.

Work circularly to make socks, sleeves, and anything else tubular, such as the Triangle Capelet on page 56.

Triangles can be made simply by increasing and decreasing. Shaped triangles are a type of bias knitting and form the basis of many shawls.

Western Auto Cowl by Carina Spencer

In knitting, the design potential of the triangle is often best captured in stranded colorwork.

Monochrome Triangle Knitted Headband and Snood by Miss Knit Nat

SQUARES

Squares can create bold designs across clothing, fashion accessories, and interiors. A square is also a basic shape found in simple garments. Try knitting a boxy pullover using a large square for the body and two smaller ones to form the sleeves.

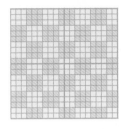

LEFT Squares are super easy to knit—just piece lots of them together for a huge geo blanket. Try out other ideas using the graph paper on page 17.

For color placement take inspiration from artists such as Sonia Delaunay, Ellsworth Kelly, and Joseph Albers, or from fashion collections.

Missoni, Spring/Summer 2016, Multicolor Square Stripe-knit Shift Dress

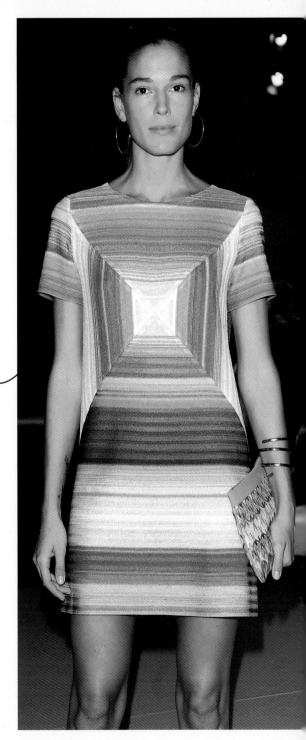

Squares can be formed in various ways. Try combining two triangles, or work from the outside edge and decrease at four points, like the cute Color Field Bag on page 72.

13

CIRCLES

Circles created with shaping are the backbone of many knitted items from shawls to tams, while stranded colorwork dots can be as simple as a single stitch forming a dot on a plain background, or larger dots charted on a graph.

Stranded colorwork circles work well with other shapes.

Lolli Knitted Scarf in Inferno Red and Seal by Seven Gauge Studios, image by Studio Photography Carmel King

Stranded knitting using two colors in a single round is most often done circularly, with the right side always facing the knitter. That way, you can watch the pattern emerge and it eliminates having to purl in the pattern, which is a tricky procedure.

CHEVRONS

The bold, geometric chevron shape is a riff on a simple diagonal stripe. The original tessellating shape, it provides bold looks and vivid, psychedelic patterns. Look for zigzags and arrow motifs in everyday life, and think about directional design when you incorporate chevrons into your work.

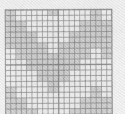

LEFT Experiment with chevrons of different widths and in different directions to create a wide range of patterns.

Bias knitting is a combination of decreasing and increasing at regular points. This technique can create chevrons. Experiment with even and uneven arrangements.

Knitted Chevron Necklace by Amy Lawrence

Chevrons can be thick or thin, garter stitch or stockinette stitch, and can have sharp points or a more serpentine shape.

Chevron Pumpkins by Erin Black

Basic chevrons in stranded knitting are formed by rearranging a diagonal stripe pattern.

Muckle Mitts by Mary Jane Mucklestone

15

EXPERIMENT WITH SHAPES

Taking your inspiration from the previous pages, try playing with different arrangements of your geometric shapes to create a whole range of geo patterns.

STRIPES, SEE PAGE 11

TRIANGLES, SEE PAGE 12

SQUARES, SEE PAGE 13

CHEVRONS, SEE PAGE 15

CHAPTER 1
THE LESSONS

Jump in and get stitching! This chapter takes you through 10 simple lessons that will have you knitting up stripes, dots, chevrons, and more in no time at all.

Each lesson is accompanied by a stylish project for you to test out your new knitting skills.

GARTER STITCH STRIPES

Knit quick and easy **garter stitch** to create bold **stripe** patterns in contrasting colors.

Stripes create a linear look that will never go out of style. They are the "neutral" of the print world, pairing easily with other patterns. Horizontal, vertical, or diagonal stripes demand attention.

In knitting, stripes are a great introduction to working with multiple colors as they can be easily mixed and stacked into interesting patterns. Garter stitch is the perfect stitch to play with this effect. Often dismissed as a beginner stitch, the distinctive 3D stripe made by garter stitch ridges can be utilized in many creative ways.

This distinctive ridged stripe, and the fantastic thick, squishy fabric it creates, comes about because garter stitch uses only one stitch—the knit stitch. Every stitch on every row is knit. Two rows of knit stitch create a ridge, which is itself a textural stripe, and continuing in the same color creates a series of horizontal ridges. Unlike some other stitch patterns, stitches in garter stitch will look the same on the front and back.

However, when garter stitch stripes are made in color, there are interesting and surprising effects. When a new color is introduced to make different colored stripes, the two sides of the fabric will look different, making a broken ridge effect that can be used as a design element when creating striped knits, as for the Möbius Cowl on page 25.

Inspiration!

Rainbow Magicowl by Elizabeth Brassard

Olana Slouch by Grace Akhrem

Varying widths can drastically alter a look.

START WITH SWATCHES

Making several generous swatches will allow you to experiment with the effects produced when knitting garter stitch stripes and will help you get to know the way the stitches work. Since garter stitch lies perfectly flat with no curling, your swatches will make perfect squares ideal for piecing into an afghan, or, when made in cotton or linen, as washcloths or dishcloths. Try knitting a plain swatch first.

TEXTURED SOLID-COLOR RIDGE STRIPES

YARN
Cascade 220 Superwash Aran, 100% Superwash Merino Wool, 3½ oz (100 g), 150 yds (137.5 m) in Deep Sea Coral

NEEDLES
US 8 (5 mm) knitting needles

1 Using long-tail method CO 30 sts.

Row 1 (RS): K.
Row 2 (WS): K.

Look at your work. See how the long-tail cast-on resembles a full garter stitch ridge from the right side? After that you've worked two rows in plain knitting, forming another ridge.

2 Rep. rows 1–2, until you have 30 ridges (56 more times).

3 Bind off. Weave in ends.

ABOVE Knit a textured solid-color ridge stripe swatch as a starting point for your experiment with garter stitch stripes.

TWO-ROW STRIPES

Now try introducing a second color. Understanding how the stripes work will help you when you want to create your own varied designs. Select two different colors of your choice for this swatch.

YARN

Cascade 220 Superwash Aran, 100% Superwash Merino Wool, 3½ oz (100 g), 150 yds (137.5 m)

Color A Deep Sea Coral

Color B Aran (Natural)

NEEDLES

US 8 (5 mm) knitting needles

RIGHT SIDE The right side of the two-row stripe swatch will have clearly defined stripes.

1 With color A, using long-tail method CO 30 sts.

Place a locking ring marker in the first or second stitch of your cast-on ridge. This will identify the front of your work.

Row 1 (RS): With color B, k.
Row 2 (WS): K.

When changing colors, always drop the working color in front and pick up the new color from behind.

Row 3 (RS): With color A, k.
Row 4 (WS): K.

2 Rep. rows 1–4 until there are 30 garter ridges (54 more rows).

3 Bind off. Weave in ends.

WRONG SIDE Notice how the wrong side of the work no longer looks the same as the front.

In a two-row or any even number repeat, the right side has clearly defined striped ridges, while the wrong side will have facing purl bumps that form flat broken stripes.

THREE-COLOR SINGLE-ROW STRIPES

Single-row stripes are most easily made with three or more colors, so you always have a new color on each edge of the fabric.

YARN

Cascade 220 Superwash Aran, 100% Superwash Merino Wool, 3½ oz (100 g), 150 yds (137.5 m)

  Color A Deep Sea Coral

  Color B Aran (Natural)

  Color C Black

NEEDLES

US 8 (5 mm) knitting needles

1 With color A, using long-tail method CO 30 sts.

Place a locking ring marker in the first or second stitch of your cast-on ridge to identify the front of your work.

Row 1 (RS): With color B, k.
Row 2 (WS): With color C, k.
Row 3 (RS): With color A, k.

2 Repeat rows 1–3, 19 times. Repeat rows 1–2 once more.

3 Bind off. Weave in ends.

RIGHT SIDE As you can see above, both the right and wrong side of this swatch look very similar, with flat broken stripes.

WRONG SIDE The three-stripe swatch therefore creates a virtually reversible fabric.

MIX THE STRIPES!

Mix up the techniques to come up with your own maverick stripe pattern! In garter stitch, a stripe with an even number of rows makes solid ridges of color. Vary the number for thick and thin stripes (see right). In uneven-row stripe patterns, the distinctive "wrong side" look will be a feature on the front of the work, as seen above.

Project

GARTER RIDGE MÖBIUS COWL

Smooth garter ridges on one side and broken color ridges on the reverse—it can be hard to choose which look you prefer. So don't! Give the piece a half twist and seam the wrong side of the bind-off edge to the front side of the cast-on edge, creating a möbius without a front or a back. The twist also allows the cowl to fit gracefully around the neck with no fuss.

BEFORE YOU BEGIN

PROJECT SPECS

FINISHED SIZE

11½" x 26" (29 cm x 66 cm)

GAUGE

17 sts x 34 rows = 4" (10 cm) square

MATERIALS

YARN

Cascade 220 Superwash Aran, 100% Superwash Merino Wool, 3½ oz (100 g), 150 yd (137.5 m)

   Color A Deep Sea Coral, 1 ball

   Color B Aran (Natural), 1 ball

NEEDLES

US 8 (5 mm) knitting needles

NOTIONS

Locking stitch marker, tapestry needle

KEY TO YARN COLORS

███ Deep Sea Coral

☐ Aran (Natural)

Stripes are most easily made with an even number of rows, because all the yarns will be attached at the same edge.

1 With color A, using long-tail method CO 45 sts.
Row 1 (RS): K.
Row 2 (WS): K.

Now look at your work. See how the long-tail cast-on resembles a full garter stitch ridge from the right side? After that you have worked two rows in plain knitting, forming another ridge in color A.

Place a locking ring marker in the first or second stitch in your cast-on ridge. This will help identify the front of your work and will remind you that this is the side that you will be joining new colors. This corner of your work will also have the tail that remains from the cast-on edge, so make sure it is not so long that you will mistake it for the strand of yarn you'll be knitting with, as that strand is connected to the ball!

2 Rep. rows 1–2, 3 times (4 ridges plus CO ridge).

Stop and look at the work again. See how the front and back of the work look almost exactly the same? Each side has horizontal ridges. The right side of the work has five horizontal ridges, because the long-tail cast-on formed a ridge. The wrong side of the work has the initial slanting stitches of the long-tail cast-on and four garter stitch ridges.

CARRYING THE YARN

Carry the yarn that is not in use carefully up the side of the work, catching it on every other row on the right side as follows: Pick up the working yarn in front and under the yarn being carried. When a new yarn is introduced, drop the old yarn in front and pick up the new yarn from behind.

3 Join color B, leaving a 6" (15 cm) tail.
Row 9 (RS): K.
Row 10 (WS): K. (one ridge in color B.)

Did you notice as you knit row 10, the wrong side of the work no longer looks the same as the front? You might already have experience with this if you practiced with swatches.

4 **Row 11:** With color A, k.
Row 12: With color A, k.
Row 13: With color B, k.
Row 14: With color B, k.
Rep. rows 11–14, 11 times.

Now you will alternate ridges in color A and color B by repeating the last four rows 11 times. When changing colors, always drop the working color in front and pick up the new color from behind. You should now have 12 garter ridges in color B.

5 From now on we'll describe our stripe sequence in ridges.
2 ridges in color A, 2 ridges in color B, 3 times.
3 ridges in color A, 3 ridges in color B, 3 times.
4 ridges in color A, 4 ridges in color B, 3 times
5 ridges in color A, 5 ridges in color B, 4 times.
Cut color B leaving a 6" (15 cm) tail.
1 ridge A.

6 Bind off. Cut yarn, leaving a 24" (60 cm) tail.

FINISHING

1 With a tapestry needle and color A, seam the wrong side of the bind-off edge to the right side of the cast-on edge using mattress stitch. Weave in ends.

STOCKINETTE STITCH STRIPES

Stockinette stitch forms the smooth and versatile fabrics that rule the runway.

From classic French sailor T-shirts to the mod '60s look of Mary Quant, most modern striped knitwear is made with stockinette stitch. This is the flexible fabric of T-shirts—a versatile stitch that provides a smooth, flat surface, giving it much more wearability than the bumpy garter stitch. Stockinette stitch is the stitch described as "plain knitting," and is created by alternating knit rows and purls rows so that only the knit stitches show on the right side of the fabric. When knitting flat, this means knitting on the right side and purling on the wrong side, but if knitting circularly, you knit every stitch on every round.

Working stripes in stockinette stitch is a joy and a delight, because the options are endless. They can be made narrow or wide, even or uneven. Work them with only two colors for a crisp graphic look or with a dozen colors in varying amounts—stripes are the perfect vehicle for using up odd balls and stray bits of yarn. When you knit for yourself you can do what you like—you make the rules! Stockinette stripes are suitable for just about any knitted item you can imagine, from garments, pullovers, cardigans, dresses, or vests to home goods such as pillows, afghans, or baby blankets. Accessories are a great place to test out stripe combinations too, such as long scarves, mittens, socks, and all kinds of hats.

Inspiration!

Delicious Knee Socks by Laura Chau

Color Blocked Nesting Bowls by Erin Black

On home goods and in fashion, stripes have impact. Adding color highlights their bold geometric look.

29

INTRODUCING STOCKINETTE STRIPES

Stockinette fabric is not reversible like garter stitch. The front is lovely, smooth, and flat while the back is bumpy with purl stitches. However, sometimes you might prefer the back side, or choose to include a bumpy purl stitch on the front of your fabric—experimentation is the key to finding the look you want. When knitting stockinette stitch stripes, you should also consider the fact that it naturally curls at the edges.

CURLING EDGES AND SELVEDGES

If you knit a swatch in plain stockinette stitch you will quickly find that the cast-on edge rolls up towards you and the side edges (selvedges) curl under. This oddity can occasionally be used as a design feature, but usually you will need to do something to combat the curling tendency. For the fabric to lie flat, the piece will need to begin with a non-curling stitch. The most common way to do this is with ribbing (see below), but any stitch pattern with a balance of knit and purl stitches could work, like seed stitch or moss stitch. A smaller needle is often used for this as well, to combat the tendency of many of these stitch patterns to grow wider than plain stockinette stitch does, and in ribbing, to help hug the body. If the selvedges of a stockinette stitch fabric are seamed, just the act of seaming will negate any need for further measures, otherwise the edges will need to be in a non-curling stitch pattern as well.

RIBBING

Ribbing is made by alternating columns of knit stitches with columns of purl stitches. It looks like textured vertical stripes—the knit stitches are smooth and prominent, while the purl stitches recede. Ribbing produces an elastic fabric, commonly used for borders, cuffs, and necklines, since the fabric will hug the body and can stretch and contract.

Most often, an even number of knit and purl stitches are used to create ribbing. K1, p1 ribbing will draw in the fabric nicely and still have a lot of stretch. K2, p2 ribbing will draw the fabric in even more, but has less "memory" and will eventually lose some of its elasticity. The more rows that you work in any ribbing, the more elastic your fabric will be and the less likely to stretch out.

Care must be taken when executing a rib. When changing from a knit stitch to a purl stitch you must bring the yarn from behind the needle toward you, to the front, to make the purl stitch. Be sure the yarn comes between the needles and not over the right hand needle, which would inadvertently make a yarn over and create both a hole and an extra stitch!

There are seemingly endless variations of ribbing, such as k2, p1 or k3, p2. Take time to try out a few and invent some of your own. Compare the elasticity and decide which you like best, and which are most suitable for your projects.

If you are working stripes in ribbing, you'll find that when you introduce a new color there is a little bump that causes the first row to have a broken appearance instead of a smooth line. Look at the swatch that shows the reverse side of stockinette and all those little purl bumps (see page 32). These purl bumps are what's showing in your ribbing. To eliminate this, introduce a new color on the right side of the work and knit every stitch of that row. On the following rows you'll resume your rib stitch pattern. This ribbing will not have as much memory as normal ribbing, but you may decide that its aesthetic appeal trumps the stretch-factor. Also, remember you can't use this method if you are changing colors on every row, because then it won't be ribbing at all!

KNITTING NEAT STRIPES

When knitting stockinette stitch stripes flat, it is easiest to work with an even number of rows for your stripes, so the yarns will all be joined on the same side of the work. When you finish one color, the previous color will be ready and waiting to be picked up. Of course you can use an uneven number of rows, just keep in mind that there will be some ends to weave in. This isn't an issue when knitting in the round, but there is another one. Knitting circularly is actually knitting in a spiral, like a candy cane. When you end the round, the first stitch of the new round sits right next to the last stitch of the previous round. Changing colors creates a little jog, and the thicker the yarn the more noticeable the jog.

The following technique will disguise the jog in the join of stripes made in circular knitting: On the second round of a new color with your right needle tip, pick up the right leg of the stitch just below the first stitch of the round and place it on the left-hand needle (this is the first stitch of the last round worked with the previous color). Knit both the first stitch of the new color and the lifted stitch of the old color together (as k2tog). Repeat these instructions for every new color stripe. If I'm making a hat, I stop using this technique when the crown shaping begins.

LEFT Knitted using super-bulky yarn this funky beanie hat is a quick and satisfying project to road test your new stockinette stitch skills. Find the full pattern on page 33.

Use ribbing, or a stitch pattern that naturally lies flat, to stop stockinette stitch items from curling at the edges.

SIMPLE STOCKINETTE STITCH SWATCH

Notice how the two sides look different and the fabric naturally curls.

YARN

Drops Karisma, 100% Wool, 1.75½ oz (50 g), 109 yds (100 m)

   Color A Bright Blue

   Color B White

NEEDLES

US 7 (4.5 mm) knitting needles

1 With color A, using long-tail method CO 30 sts.

Row 1 (RS): K.
Row 2 (WS): P.

2 Rep. rounds 1–2 a further four times. Cut color A.

For the remainder of the swatch you will be working in stockinette stitch, alternating knit and purl rows.

3 Join color B. Work 6 rows.

4 Join color A. Work 2 rows.

5 Carry color B carefully up the side, being careful not to pull too tightly. Work 6 rows color B.

6 Join color A. Work 2 rows.

7 Work 2 rows color B.

8 Work 8 rows color A.

9 Bind off. Weave in ends.

RIGHT SIDE This swatch has been steamed. Beforehand, both the cast-on and bind-off edges curled up, while the side edges curled under.

WRONG SIDE The wrong side of the simple stockinette stitch swatch will look different from the right site, with broken stripes.

Project

CHUNKY STOCKINETTE STRIPED BEANIE

Ward off the cold with a fast and furious knit beanie in super-bulky yarn. This hat is knitted flat, beginning with several rows of ribbing to hug the head, before moving on to wide stockinette stitch stripes. Simple shaping after the stripes creates the curve of the crown, and with careful seaming the stripes will match up perfectly.

BEFORE YOU BEGIN

PROJECT SPECS

FINISHED SIZE

17¾" (45 cm) circumference with 1–2" of negative ease

GAUGE

Unblocked: 7½ sts x 11 rows = 4" (10 cm) square in stockinette stitch

Blocked: 7½ sts x 10½ rows = 4" (10 cm) square in stockinette stitch

MATERIALS

YARN

Wool and the Gang Crazy Sexy Wool, 100% Wool, 7 oz (200 g), 87 yds (80 m)

    Color A Tweed Gray, 1 ball

    Color B Magic Mint, 1 ball

NEEDLES

US 17 (12.75 mm) knitting needles

NOTIONS

Locking stitch marker, tapestry needle, pom-pom maker (or cardboard and scissors)

KEY TO YARN COLORS

■	Tweed Gray
■	Magic Mint

1 With color A, using long-tail method CO 32 sts.

You might want to place a locking stitch marker to indicate the right side of your work here.

2 Work 4 rows in k1, p1 rib stitch.

You'll notice when working on the right side or wrong side in ribbing, you will always be knitting into the knit stitch of the previous row, and always purling into the purl stitch of the previous row.

3 Join color B, leaving a 6" (15 cm) tail.
Row 1 (RS): K.
Row 2 (WS): P.
Row 3: K.
Row 4: P.

For the remainder of the beanie you will be working in stockinette stitch. When joining the new yarn, I just begin knitting with the new color, leaving a tail long enough to weave in later. Some people find it more comfortable to tie the old color to the new color with a loose knot that will be easy to undo when the time comes to weave in the ends.

At the start of row 3, loosely pull the color A strand up the side edge of the work, and capture it by bringing the working yarn, color B, in front of it. That way it will be in the right place when it's time to use it again, and you'll be less likely to pull it too tight.

4 Work 2 rows color A.
Row 1: K.
Row 2: P.

Pick up color A from where you trapped it and begin knitting, taking care not to pull too tightly.

5 Work 4 rows color B.

A NOTE ON GAUGE

If you get more stitches/rows than the pattern gauge, it means your knitting is tighter—try going up a needle size. If you get fewer stitches/rows than the pattern gauge, your knitting is looser—try going down a needle size. Sometimes, large needles are not easy to replace as yarn shops don't always have a wide variety. In that case, you can try making small adjustments in your knitting style to get the correct gauge. Try and knit tighter by pulling on the yarn a little more fiercely, or for a looser gauge try relaxing your grip a bit.

6 Work 4 rows color A.

Trap color B on the edge of the second RS row as before.

Cut color A, leaving a 6" (15 cm) tail.

7 Work 4 rows color B.

CROWN SHAPING

1 Row 1 (DECREASE ROW): *K2, k2tog; rep. from * 8 times.
24 sts.
Row 2: P.
Row 3 (DECREASE ROW): *K1, k2tog; rep. from * 8 times. 16 sts.
Row 4: P.
Row 5 (DECREASE ROW): *K2tog; rep. from * 8 times. 8 sts.

Carefully spaced decreases will shape the crown of the hat, so that when seamed it will form an elegant dome.

2 Cut yarn leaving an 8" (20 cm) tail. Thread tail through last 8 sts. Fasten off.

FINISHING

1 With tapestry needle and color B, sew side seams together using mattress stitch. Weave in ends.

You will need about 15" (38 cm) of color B to sew the seams together. Take your time, making sure the stripes match. Loosely-spun single-ply wool can be tricky to sew with, so have patience and persevere!

2 Make a giant 4" (10 cm) pom-pom in whichever color you prefer.

See page 138 for details on how to make your pom-pom. Once made, secure your pom-pom to the top of the hat using the tapestry needle. Use the long tails from tying the pom-pom to sew it firmly in place on top of the beanie. Weave in ends.

DIAGONAL COLORWORK STRIPES

Stranded colorwork is the key to bright and bold patterned knitting.

What do you think of when you imagine stranded colorwork? Reindeer holiday knits, patterned yokes on Icelandic sweaters, and the highly patterned horizontal bands on Fair Isle vests? All of these are knit with the colorwork technique called stranded knitting, but this ubiquitous knitting is also found in most fashion and sportswear collections, no matter the season.

Stranded colorwork differs from the intarsia technique, which has separate areas of color as a shape against a plain background. In stranded colorwork, two or more colors are used in a single round of knitting. The colors are used the entire way around the garment, so a pattern (usually a repeat pattern) encircles it. Stranded colorwork allows for a huge variety of patterns and provides opportunities to use colors in bold and bright ways.

Though it seems complicated at first, knitting with two colors isn't difficult. There are several things you need to learn at once though, so go easy on yourself if you don't master them all right away—it takes practice! Traditional stranded colorwork is almost always knit in the round, because when you knit circularly, the right side of your work is always facing you and you can watch the color patterns emerge. Geometric patterns can provide a brilliant introduction to stranded colorwork, because the symmetry makes it easy to anticipate how the pattern will look, and also makes them simple to memorize. Patterns will look different just by altering your choice of colors too, so there is plenty of room for experimentation.

Inspiration!

Fishbones by Mary Jane Mucklestone

From Berroco Portfolio Vol.1, photo courtesy of Berroco

Amazing Maze Scarf by Sarah Elwick Knitwear

Once you know what to look for, you'll find stranded colorwork every season in most fashion collections.

INTRODUCING STRANDED COLORWORK

To master stranded colorwork knitting, you'll need to learn to hold and work with two colors of yarn at the same time, alternating the colors used for the stitches. The yarn not in use is stranded across the back of the fabric—these are the floats. The best way to learn this is simply to practice—with time you will get the hang of it! You will also need to learn to read charts. Instead of colorwork instructions being written out in words, charts are given, providing a visual guide to the pattern.

READING CHARTS

Knitting charts are presented on a square grid or graph, where each square represents a single stitch. Every horizontal row of squares indicates a row of the pattern, which will be repeated the number of times required to circle your garment. Each chart usually represents an entire single pattern motif, which also will be repeated for the number of times required to complete your garment. When knitting circularly, read the chart from right to left, and bottom to top. Circular knitting charts are numbered up the right side, indicating the round number. Take a look at page 115 for in-depth instructions on how to read charts.

FAIR ISLE KNITTING

Fair Isle knitting is a very specific regional style of stranded knitting that was developed on Fair Isle, one of the Scottish Shetland Islands. Traditional Fair Isle knitting is stranded knitting, worked in the round, with never more than two colors in a single round. It should be knit from yarn produced in Shetland, from the wool of the Shetland breed of sheep. It is a sophisticated style, which produces some of the most fantastic color effects, offering subtle shadings or a riot of color.

Fair Isle garments are often made up of horizontal bands, sporting larger and smaller motifs; border patterns and peerie patterns respectively. The pattern motifs themselves are usually geometric, with four or more lines of symmetry, making them easy to memorize. Motifs usually have no more than an inch, or about eight stitches, between color changes to avoid long floats.

RIGHT Diagonal lines can be arranged to make bold chevron patterns.

In this chart and the chart below, a single pattern motif or repeat is outlined in red and multiple pattern repeats are shown in order to illustrate the appearance of the final knitted fabric.

RIGHT Flip your pattern to create vertical zigzag lines.

VERSATILE CHARTS

The small six-stitch by six-row pattern motif for the tablet cover in this lesson creates diagonal stripes when repeated (see page 40). Small pattern elements like this are fun to work with, because there are so many possibilities. Different arrangements of the same pattern elements make very different results. Stack this little pattern and flip it periodically for zigzags, and turn the zigzags on their sides for chevrons. Flip half the zigzag, eliminate a row and another bird's eye pattern motif emerges!

LEFT You can arrange diagonal lines in any number of ways, flipping, stacking, and rotating to create different designs such as this bird's eye pattern.

EXPERIMENT WITH CHARTS

Cast on a multiple of the smallest pattern element, outlined in red, and practice knitting these patterns yourself. To make it easier, make sure you have enough stitches to comfortably fit around a 16" (40 cm) circular needle. Begin with a non-curling edge like a k1, p1 rib for about an inch before you begin the colorwork. Stranded colorwork is often tighter than ordinary stockinette stitch, so you may choose a needle larger than normal.

CORRUGATED RIBBING

Polarized Hat by Tanis Gray

Vertical stripes worked in ribbing are often used as decorative edgings for borders, cuffs, and necklines. Called corrugated ribbing, it is created by keeping the knit stitches of the ribbing in one color and the purl stitches in another. All the knit stitches may be a single color and all the purl stitches another single color, however they are often both changed every few rounds allowing room to experiment. Corrugated ribbing is most often worked over an even number of stitches, usually k2, p2 or k1, p1. Due to the stranding, it is not as elastic as ordinary ribbing. If you wanted to go stripe-crazy, you could knit the ribbing for the iPad case like this too!

1 With color A (lighter color), k 2 sts.

2 Bring color B (darker color) forward, p 2 sts.

3 Bring the yarn back and start again.

When introducing a new color, there will be a bi-colored purl bump, which can be a nice design element. If you'd rather have a smooth transition, knit every stitch in the round where the new color is introduced just as in regular striped ribbing. This will affect the flexibility of the ribbing a bit, making it even less stretchy. Of course you will not want to change colors on every round, or it would not be ribbing at all!

DIAGONAL STRIPED TABLET CASE

This cute tablet case is the perfect first project for stranded colorwork, because there are just three stitches of one color before you change and knit three stitches of another, meaning the floats are never very long. You will also practice ribbing, make simple buttonholes, and work a three-needle bind-off. In this project you will work in the round, so you will always be working on the right side.

BEFORE YOU BEGIN

PROJECT SPECS

FINISHED SIZE

15" circumference x 11½" height, including button band (38 cm x 29.5 cm)

GAUGE

19 sts x 24 rounds = 4" (10 cm) square in colorwork pattern

MATERIALS

YARN

Cascade Yarns 220 Superwash Aran, 100% Superwash Merino Wool, 3½ oz (100 g), 150 yds (137.5 m)

    Color A Magenta, 1 ball

    Color B Black, 1 ball

    Color C White, 1 ball

NEEDLES

US 7 (4.5 mm) circular needle, 16" (40 cm) length

US 7 (4.5 mm) knitting needles

US 8 (5 mm) knitting needles

NOTIONS

Stitch marker, tapestry needle, 3 x ⅞" (20 mm) buttons

Optional: An extra needle in size US 7 (4.5 mm) and US 8 (5 mm), straight or dpn. An extra needle is needed to work a three-needle bind-off

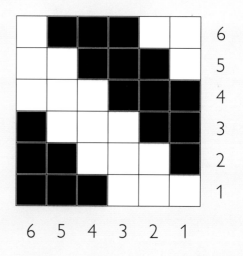

KEY TO YARN COLORS

⬛	Magenta
⬛	Black
⬜	White

RIBBING BAND

1 With the smaller needle and color A, using long-tail method CO 72 sts.

Place a stitch marker and join for working in the round, taking care not to twist the stitches. The marker indicates the beginning of the round. Take great care when you join your cast-on stitches. Make sure the base of all of the cast stitches are facing towards your body and place a marker over the needle point in the right hand. Join by inserting the right-hand needle point into the first stitch on the left-hand needle point and begin knitting. Extra time spent making sure the cast-on is not twisted is well spent. Imagine your distress after knitting the ribbing to find that you've inadvertently knit a möbius!

2 ROUNDS 1–3: K1, p1.

3 ROUND 4 (BUTTONHOLE ROUND 1).

Work 5 sts in k1, p1 rib (k1, p1, k1, p1, k1). BO 2 sts (p1, k1, pass the purl stitch over the last knit stitch. P1, pass the knit stitch over the last purled stitch).

First buttonhole placed.

Work 9 sts in k1, p1 rib (*k1, p1; rep. from * 4 times, end k1). BO 2 sts (p1, k1, pass the purl stitch over the last knit stitch. P1, pass the knit stitch over the last purled stitch).

Second buttonhole placed.

Work 9 sts in k1, p1 rib (*k1, p1; rep. from * 4 times, end k1). BO 2 sts (p1, k1, pass the purl stitch over the last knit stitch. P1, pass the knit stitch over the last purled stitch).

Third buttonhole placed.

K1, p1, rib to end of round.

A NOTE ON GAUGE

In this pattern the stitch gauge is more important than the round gauge. Matching the stitch gauge will give you the correct circumference. Since it is an allover pattern repeat, you can easily add or subtract rounds to get the correct finished length.

4 ROUND 5 (BUTTONHOLE ROUND 2).

Work 5 stitches in k1, p1 rib (k1, p1, k1, p1, k1).
With backward loop method, CO 2 sts.

First buttonhole finished.

Work 10 sts in k1, p1 rib (*p1, k1; rep. from * 5 times).
With backward loop method, CO 2 sts.

Second buttonhole finished.

Work 10 sts in k1, p1 rib (*p1, k1; rep. from * 5 times).
With backward loop method, CO 2 sts.

Third buttonhole finished.

Work k1, p1 rib to end of round (P1, *k1 p1; rep. from * to end of round).

5 ROUNDS 6 AND 7: K1, p1 rib.

Ribbing band finished.

Cut color A, leaving a 6" (15 cm) tail.

MAIN CASE

1 Change to larger needle. With color B, k1 round.

Using color B, begin knitting onto the larger needle. Make sure you still have your marker at the beginning of the round!

2 Begin the stranded colorwork pattern. Work 6 sts of colorwork chart, 12 times.

Read the chart from the bottom right corner moving left across the chart, just as the knitting is knit. On round 1 you will knit three stitches in white, followed by three stitches in black, and after you have worked the sixth pattern stitch, the pattern begins again at stitch number one. You will repeat these six stitches over and over until you have completed the round.

Strand the color not in use smoothly across the wrong side, neither too tightly (causing the fabric to pucker) nor too loosely (creating loops of yarn).

To make sure that the strands of yarn not in use are long enough, spread your just-knit stitches along the right-hand needle.

When you reach the end of the round, move on to round 2 of the chart, again reading from right to left. One stitch color B, three stitches color C, two stitches color B, and repeat. You will quickly see that the pattern is still alternating three stitches of white with three stitches of black, but it has started one stitch over, creating a diagonal leaning to the left. It will take six rounds until you need to begin round 1 again.

3 Work until piece measures 11½" (29 cm) from beginning.

Cut color C.
With color B, k 1 round.

THREE-NEEDLE BIND-OFF

Now you will work a three-needle bind off. With the stitches still on the needle, turn the work inside out so that the wrong side is facing you.

1 Remove the marker. Keep the first 36 sts on the left-hand point of the needle, slide the last 36 sts to the other point of the needle.

The cable will extend between the two groups of stitches. Line up both ends of the needle so that they are parallel, with the stitches at the points. Hold both needles in your left hand.

2 With the third needle (RH), k into the first st on each needle.

Make a stitch. You will now have one stitch on the right-hand needle.

3 Rep. step 3.

You now have two stitches on the right-hand needle.

4 Take the first st on RH needle and pass it over the last st.

One stitch bound off.

5 Rep. steps 3–5 until 1 st remains on RH needle.

6 Cut yarn.

Pull the tail through the last stitch to fasten off.

FINISHING

1 Weave in ends.

2 Block so the piece is flat.

Take care that the ribbing is neatly folded with the three buttonholes centered. Allow to dry.

3 Sew buttons on the inside of the ribbing beneath the buttonholes.

I use a tapestry needle threaded with a contrasting color and make a tiny stitch to mark where I want to place the button. To sew the button on to the fabric, I will often use standard sewing thread because the openings on many buttons are too small to accommodate yarn.

SOMETHING LOOKS OFF?

When you reach the beginning of the round it may seem like the pattern is off. This is because the charts are written as if each round is a circle or a disc stacked like plates on top of one another. However, because circular knitting is actually a spiral, the pattern will not match up perfectly at the join. It is a handmade object and no one will notice this join. It occurs where a seam might otherwise be, on the edge of the tablet case.

GARTER STITCH TRIANGLES

Shaping your knits on the bias with increases and decreases will produce instant geometric **triangles**.

It's easy and fun to create geometric triangles simply by shaping the fabric itself with strategically placed increases and decreases. Shaping your knits in this way creates what is called a bias fabric, because the work grows from the corners out on the diagonal—or on the "bias." Triangles are the first shapes you will create in this way. They are the foundation for traditional shawls found all over the world and form the backbone of many afghan patterns. Once, while sailing, I quickly knit two triangles for a swimsuit top when I discovered I'd forgotten mine— you might just dream up some clever ideas of your own!

Garter stitch is a great stitch for triangle-shaped pieces, since it lays flat and does not curl. To make triangles, we begin with a small number of stitches for the first corner, and by increasing every other row, create a 90-degree angle with two equal sides. It's easy to customize these simple triangles, and they can be used to make all sorts of patterns and shapes. For example, slowing down the rate of increases will give an elongated triangle. Putting two triangles together will form a square, or, instead of making two triangles and sewing them together, you can simply continue knitting, replacing the increases with decreases and working towards the opposite corner to create a full square.

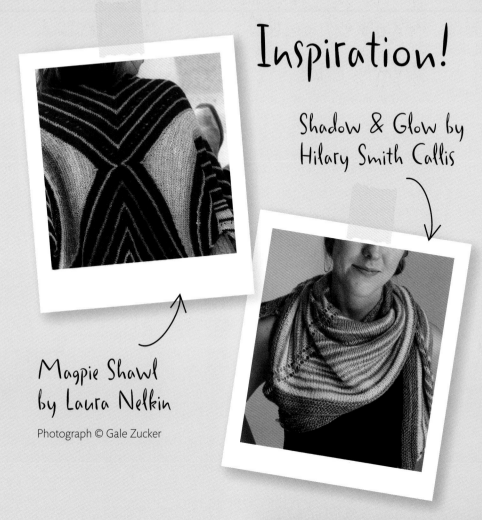

Inspiration!

Shadow & Glow by Hilary Smith Callis

Magpie Shawl by Laura Nelkin

Photograph © Gale Zucker

Traditional Icelandic shawls begin with a small number of stitches with paired increases at the edges and the center, creating two triangles.

START WITH SWATCHES

Knit these swatches to practice your increases and decreases. These swatches can also be pieced together into an afghan, used as pretty dishcloths, or hung up as a string of pennants. There are basic instructions here, with specific ways of increasing, but make a few swatches and experiment with the different increase methods found at the back of the book to decide which is your favorite (see pages 120–121). Try changing colors and adding stripes, too.

WHAT ARE M1R AND M1L?

There are several different ways to increase or make an extra stitch. In fine knitwear, elegant balanced increases occur in pairs with one leaning to the right and the other to the left. Clever needle maneuvering or a simple backward loop placed on the right hand needle achieve similar results. You can try out this technique when increasing on each edge of your triangle afghan and pennant swatches, for a nearly invisible increase. See pages 120-121 for more details.

Look to classic quilt placement patterns for inspiration when putting together an afghan. Remember to consider color choice too—this can drastically alter the look of your piece.

SIMPLE AFGHAN SQUARE

Work increases and decreases on right-side rows to create a triangle that ends with a square! Make a stack of these squares and build an afghan, playing with the arrangement for different geometric effects.

These swatches are worked in two colors to clearly illustrate the triangle shapes, but you could just as easily make every square different. Studying quilts is a great way to understand the different placement possibilities of these squares.

YARN

Berroco Vintage, 52% Acrylic, 40% Wool, 8% Nylon, 3½ oz (100 g), 217 yds (198 m)

Color A Orange

Color B Mochi

NEEDLES

US 7 (4.5 mm) knitting needles

1 With color A, using long-tail method CO 3 sts.

Row 1 (WS): K.
Row 2 (increase row, RS): K1, m1R, k to last st, m1L, k1.

2 Rep. rows 1–2 until you have 33 sts, ending on a WS row.

3 Cut yarn. Weave in ends. Do not remove the stitches from the needle.

Now create a square by making a triangle in the other direction.

4 Join Color B.

Row 1 (decrease row, RS): K1, ssk, k to 3 sts before the end of the row, k2tog, k1.
Row 2: K.

5 Rep. rows 1–2 until 5 sts remain.

Next row: Ssk, k1, k2tog.
Next row: K 3 sts.

6 Cut yarn and draw through the loops. Weave in ends.

CHEERFUL PENNANTS

Knitting more rows between increases will form an elongated triangle. Knitting lots of these cute triangles in a variety of colors and yarns is quick and easy practice, and will also show you just how easy it is to make different shapes by altering a few stitches here and there. Afterward, you'll have enough triangles to make a homemade string of pennants.

YARN

Berroco Vintage, 52% Acrylic, 40% Wool, 8% Nylon, 3½ oz (100 g), 217 yds (198 m)

    Color A Blue Note

    Color B Petunia

    Color C Wild Blueberry

NEEDLES

US 7 (4.5 mm) knitting needles

An isosceles triangle is easily knit in garter stitch by beginning at one point and increasing on each edge every other row.

1 Using long-tail method, CO 3 sts.

Rows 1–3: K.
Row 4: K1, m1R, k to last st, m1L, k1.

2 Rep. rows 1–4 until you have 33 sts.

3 Bind off. Weave in ends.

Sew onto ribbon, or thread a sturdy yarn or string through the top, and hang from the rafters!

PENNANT SWATCHES These cheerful little triangles can be placed in any number of different arrangements to make bold patterns.

TRADITIONAL GRANNY'S DISHCLOTH

My 90-year-old neighbor Frances made these simple squares by the dozen and sold them at her year-round yard sale. They can be used for much more than doing dishes—you might be surprised to find what a welcome gift they can be. They are traditionally made with old-fashioned cotton yarn, specifically Lily Sugar N' Cream, as used below; using a fairly large needle such as US 8 (5 mm). However, I like to make them in linen or hemp so they're a little exfoliating—paired with a bar of homemade soap, you've got an indulgent spa-themed gift. The construction of this popular pattern is simple, with increases and decreases worked at the beginning of every row.

YARN

Lily Sugar N'Cream, worsted weight 100% cotton yarn, 2 oz (71 g), 120 yds (109 m)

NEEDLES

US 8 (5 mm) knitting needles

1 Using long-tail method, CO 4 sts.

Row 1: K.
Row 2: K2, yo, k to end of row.

2 Rep. row 2 until there are 44 sts.

3 NEXT ROW: K1, k2tog, yo, k2tog, k to end.

Rep. last row until 4 sts remain.

4 Bind off. Weave in ends.

GRANNY'S DISHCLOTH These dishcloth swatches are simple to knit up and can make a lovely gift.

HAPS

A "hap" is a word in Shetland dialect that as a noun refers to a hand-knitted shawl worked in coarse everyday wool. This is in contrast to the fine lace shawls that the islands are famous for. As a verb, the word hap means to enfold or cover. In knitting terms, a hap is even more specific. A Shetland hap shawl is composed of three parts: a square garter stitch center (often knit on the diagonal like the afghan square, opposite), a fairly wide simple lace border, and a small lace edging. A half hap has a triangle center.

Project

TRIANGULAR GARTER STITCH SHAWL

This elegant scarf is an interpretation of a classic Icelandic shawl, using gradient colors to create a subtle chevron at the base. This arrangement is also the perfect blank canvas for inserting lace patterns.

BEFORE YOU BEGIN

PROJECT SPECS

FINISHED SIZE

43¾" x 20½" (111 cm x 52 cm)

GAUGE

Unblocked: 17 sts x 34 rows = 4" (10 cm) square in garter stitch

Blocked: approx. 16 sts x 24 rows = 4" (10 cm) square in garter stitch

The blocked gauge will vary slightly across the project.

MATERIALS

YARN

Malabrigo Silky Merino, 50% silk, 50% merino, 1¾ oz (50 g), 150 yds (137 m)

　Color A Matisse Blue, 1 ball

　Color B Azul Azul, 1 ball

NEEDLES

US 8 (5 mm) circular needle, 24" (60 cm) length

NOTIONS

Stitch markers, tapestry needle

KNITTING FLAT WITH CIRCULAR NEEDLES

This project requires a circular needle, but is knit back and forth in rows. A circular needle can accommodate the many stitches a shawl requires.

KEY TO YARN COLORS

■	Matisse Blue
■	Azul

1 With color A, using long-tail method CO 9 sts.

SET-UP ROW: K3, pm, k3, pm, k to end.

"Pm" indicates where you should place a marker. These markers isolate the center three stitches of the shawl. You will increase on either side of these stitches, and at the same time increase on both outside edges every right-side row. This will form two triangles, that together form one large triangle. I also find it useful to place a marker to indicate the right side of the work, to know at a glance if it is an increase row or not.

2 Row 1 (RS): K2, yo, k to marker, yo, sl marker, k3, sl marker, yo, k to last 2 sts, yo, k2. 4 sts increased.

3 Row 2 (WS): K.

4 Rep. rows 1–2 to end of yarn.

Cut yarn leaving 6" (15 cm) tail.

5 Join color B and rep. rows 1–2 until you have 241 sts on the needle after working a WS row.

This is 119 stitches, plus the three center stitches, and another 119 stitches. The border will need to be multiple of three, plus four.

NEARLY INVISIBLE JOIN

Try this trick for joining a new color yarn: When you reach the edge where the color is to change, cut the old yarn leaving a 1" (2.5 cm) tail. Un-knit about 10–12 stitches. Spit splice the new yarn to the old yarn (see page 135). Resume knitting, and the new color should start around the end of the row.

AUTHENTIC SHAPE

The cast-on edge of this shawl has a slight scoop where the original nine stitches are cast on. This is natural and a typical feature of traditional Icelandic shawls, but you can easily make it disappear with careful blocking.

BORDER

1 Row 1 (RS): K2, * yo, k2tog, k1; rep. from * until middle 3 sts, yo, K3; **yo, k2tog, k1; rep. from ** until 2 sts remain, end yo, k2.

2 Row 2 (WS): K.

3 Row 3 (RS): K.

Bind off loosely.

FINISHING

1 Weave in ends.

2 Block to triangle shape.

STRANDED COLORWORK TRIANGLES

Unlock the potential of **triangle** shapes with dynamic **colorwork**.

Triangles are the backbone for many traditional knits, but this versatile shape will pop up everywhere once you start looking for it. As one of the foundations of graphic design, triangles are found all over the world in every imaginable medium: from tile work, wood flooring, and glass mosaics to rug patterns, woven coverlets, printed fabric, and architecture. As a repeating pattern motif, triangles are pleasingly simple yet hold innumerable design possibilities. Observe how placing a triangle in a different orientation can completely change its effect, and notice how triangles of different sizes can be used in a single pattern repeat.

In knitting, the design possibilities of triangles are best captured in stranded colorwork, where the flat surface and opportunity for color ensure a dynamic composition. These simple shapes and patterns can be incorporated into a wide variety of knitted items. Take inspiration from the triangles you see in daily life to design your own triangular patterns. Do you prefer simple symmetrical stacking of a repeated equilateral triangle, or various sizes of triangles over several rows? When designing, always keep in mind the level of difficulty you feel comfortable with in your knitting. You may be tempted to design very large triangles, but remember that with them come very long floats for you to manage!

Inspiration!

Convertible Triangle Color Blocked Bowl by Erin Black

Flying Geese Cowl by Mary Jane Mucklestone

Analyze triangle repeat patterns and notice the negative and positive areas in designs.

DESIGNING WITH TRIANGLES

The charts on these pages all begin with a similar triangle shape, but moving them around can create very different graphic designs. The addition of color further changes the look of a pattern, sometimes making it almost unrecognizable to another that uses the same motif! This proves that designs needn't be overly complex—endless variations exist from using the same simple shapes.

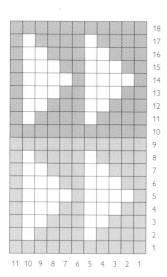

CHANGING DIRECTIONS
In the charts to the left and below left, we have the same triangle in both stitch patterns. The chart to the left has the triangles pointing to the right, while below they are pointing up. By simply rotating the pattern, we can make a very different design.

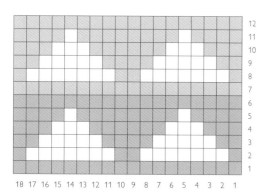

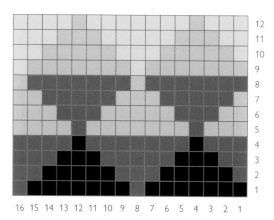

CREATIVE COLOR Color choice is important for all geometric patterns, but particularly triangles, as it can transform the pattern you create. Simply changing the color of the triangles can give the exact same pattern repeat a totally different look, as shown in the two charts above.

When looking at design ideas outside of knitting, remember that in a beginner's stranded knitting pattern, no more than two colors will ever be used in a single round. You can gain inspiration for color from complex design, but you won't necessarily be able to use the same color arrangement. Instead, use it to inspire your own design.

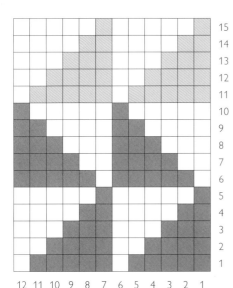

15
14
13
12
11
10
9
8
7
6
5
4
3
2
1

12 11 10 9 8 7 6 5 4 3 2 1

CHOOSING COLOR The same triangle shapes in different orientations, combined with a contrasting placement of color, can create strikingly different looks. Try stacking your pattern repeats and colors in different ways to create sawtooth, zigzag, or stripe effects.

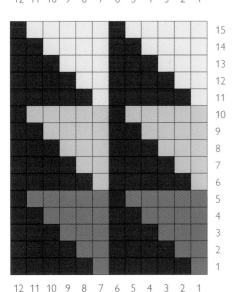

15
14
13
12
11
10
9
8
7
6
5
4
3
2
1

12 11 10 9 8 7 6 5 4 3 2 1

STEEKING

Circular knitting, or knitting "in the round" creates a seamless tubular fabric that can form the basis of many garments—sweaters, hats, mittens, gloves, socks, and skirts, for example. The bodies of sweaters and cardigans need openings for necklines, sleeves, and front openings. When knitting with more than one color in a round, or stranded knitting, making these openings requires steeks, which are extra stitches used to bridge the gap where an opening is needed, allowing you to continue knitting in the round. All the colors used in the round will be alternated within the steek. When the knitting is complete, these extra stitches are cut down the center with sharp scissors, creating an opening where sleeves may be attached or a neck edging or button band picked up. We don't use this advanced technique in this book, but you might encounter it in future circular knitting projects.

The Fair Isle Vest by Mary Jane Mucklestone; image by Carrie Bostick Hoge

TRIANGLE CAPELET

Capelets provide more warmth than a scarf, but are easier to wear than a shawl. They're great for layering-up over fine sweaters or soft cardigans, and the neutral palette of this design makes it easy to pair with other items. A simply stranded pattern of white triangles against alternating gray and fawn backgrounds makes this easy to memorize, too. The capelet is worked in the round from the bottom up, with the triangles gradually diminishing in size and ending with a relaxed ribbed cowl neck that can be worn up or folded over. It is a perfect project to expand your colorwork horizons and a good step to take before attempting to knit something more adventurous, like a colorwork sweater.

BEFORE YOU BEGIN

PROJECT SPECS

FINISHED SIZE

Extra small (small, medium, large, extra large): 41¾ (44½, 47¼, 52⅜, 55⅛)" [106 (113, 120, 133, 140) cm] shoulder circumference.

GAUGE

Blocked: 16 sts x 19 rounds = 4" (10 cm)

MATERIALS

YARN

Cascade Yarn Eco Cloud, 70% Undyed Merino Wool, 30% Undyed Baby Alpaca, 3½ oz (100 g) 164 yds (150 m)

   Color A Dove Gray, 2 (2, 2, 3, 4) balls

   Color B Cream, 1 (1, 1, 2, 3) ball

   Color C Bunny, 1 (1, 1, 2, 2) ball

NEEDLES

US 10 (6 mm) circular needles, 24" (60 cm) length

US 9 (5.5 mm) circular needle, 16" (40 cm) length

NOTIONS

Stitch marker, tapestry needle

KEY TO YARN COLORS

▨	Dove Gray
☐	Cream
▧	Bunny

C

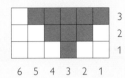

6 5 4 3 2 1

B

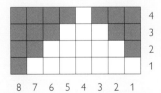

8 7 6 5 4 3 2 1

A

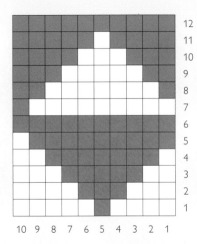

10 9 8 7 6 5 4 3 2 1

1 With color A and larger needle, using cable method CO 160 (170, 180, 200, 210) sts.

The simple cable cast-on is loosely made so that the capelet is soft and flexible. You might want to go up a needle size if your cast-on stitches are typically tight.

Place marker and join without twisting for working in the round.

Stranded colorwork is easiest when worked in the round. Take care when you join your cast-on stitches. Make sure the base of the cast-on is facing towards your body and place a marker over the needle point in the right hand. Join by working the needle into the first stitch on the left-hand needle point.

2 Work k1, p1 rib for about 2" (5 cm).

A simple rib at the beginning keeps the edge from curling up on itself.

3 Work rounds 1–12 of colorwork chart A 2 (2, 3, 3, 4) times and rounds 1–5 of colorwork chart A once more.

Now is the time to analyze the chart. Determine which stitches are the background color (gray boxes and brown boxes) and which are the pattern color (white boxes). Read the chart from the bottom right corner moving left across the chart, just as the knitting is knit. When you reach the tenth pattern stitch, begin again at stitch number one. Keep repeating these same 10-stitches around the piece, changing the background after every sixth round as indicated.

4 NEXT ROUND (DECREASE ROUND): With color A, k2, *ssk, k1, k2tog, k5; rep. from * 15 (16, 17, 19, 20) times, ssk, k1, k2tog, k3. 128 (136, 144, 160, 168) sts.

To make things easier, the chart is broken down into three parts: A, B, and C. As the shaping is only done in plain rounds with one color, dividing the charts this way is logical.

SOMETHING LOOKS OFF?

When you reach the beginning again, the pattern will seem to be "off." Never fear—circular knitting is a spiral, so a chart representation will always be off at this point. That is just the way it is, no need to fret. It's nice to have a handmade capelet and no one will notice this join.

5 Work rounds 1–4 of colorwork chart B.

Notice that now there is now a repeat of eight stitches.

6 DECREASE ROUND: With color B, *k2tog, k3, ssk, k1; rep from * 16 (17, 18, 20, 21) times. 96 (102, 108, 120, 126) sts.

7 Work rounds 1–3 of colorwork chart C.

Notice that now there is a repeat of six stitches.

Cut color C, leaving a 6" (15 cm) tail.

8 With color A, k1 round.

9 DECREASE ROUND: K 0 (3, 0, 0, 3), *k6 (6, 7, 8, 8), k2tog; rep. from * 12 times, k0 (3, 0, 0, 3). 84 (90, 96, 108, 114) sts.

10 Change to smaller needle. In color A, work k1, p1 rib for about 8" (20 cm) or to the desired depth in color A.

This step is included to make the neckline ribbing draw in a little more than the cast-on edge, which should be a little more flexible. Start knitting from the old larger needle onto the new smaller needle as you knit the first round of final ribbing.

11 Bind off.

As with the cast-on, make sure that the bind-off is flexible and not too tight. I bind off in the ribbing pattern itself, because I like a bit of a crinkly edge!

FINISHING

1 Weave in ends.

2 Block, gently shaping.

You can decide how you prefer the neck to fit. If you like a wide-ribbed neck, as shown, block it accordingly. If you prefer a tight neck—more of a turtle neck—you can block it as small and tight as you can!

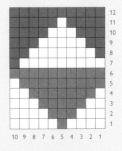

COLOR CUSTOMIZATION

Customize your capelet with color! Try changing the background colors, so that instead of alternating gray and brown, the background is worked in a gradient from dark up to light. Or, go for a bold graphic style with a solid background throughout and substitute the white pattern triangles with high-contrasting accent colors—a rainbow selection perhaps—swapping the color of the pattern triangle each time a new one begins. Remember though, each horizontal band of triangles will only have two colors, to make the work simple. You might also consider choosing a variegated yarn as one of your two colors. Just make sure there is enough color contrast with your background yarn throughout the variation. Likewise, if you want to try two variegated yarns, they must have very high contrast for the triangle patterns to show.

C

Refer to the charts as instructed in the pattern.

B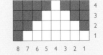

A

59

MITERED SQUARES

Develop your pattern-play skills with clever bias knit **mitered squares**.

Squares and rectangles, are the most basic shapes in fashion. Many traditional garments and ancient costumes from around the world use this geometric shape as their basis. This makes perfect sense, because a loom produces a square or rectangular cloth. The less cutting that is done, the less waste, both in the fabric itself and the labor involved in making it. Think of togas and kilts, which are long rectangles cleverly gathered to form garments.

You can play with square shapes by making mitered squares. They are a type of bias knitting, sometimes called domino knitting, with an ingenious way of producing a square shape. With diagonal garter stitch, which is also bias knitting, you saw how squares can be built by starting at a corner, increasing to the middle, and then decreasing back down to the opposite corner. This time, for mitered squares, you will cast on the total number of stitches at the very beginning, and decrease at the center to form a square. Although it is a very specific technique not really found outside of knitting, the addition of color and the arrangement of the squares echoes quilting, tile work, and other graphic design based on a square. Mitered squares make the perfect base for blankets and cushions, but some knitwear designers have come up with ways to fashion beautiful shawls and even garments from them.

COLOR INSPIRATION

Mitered squares are a fantastic medium to experiment with bold color placement. Look to artists Ellsworth Kelly and Joseph Albers for inspiration, as well as the fascinating Sonia Delaunay, who combined a life in fine art with an influential fashion business.

Inspiration!

Mitered Square Blanket by Kay Gardiner and Ann Shayne
Photograph © Steve Gross and Sue Daley

Mitre Shona Long Jacket by Jane Slicer-Smith

In garter stitch, the number of stitches in a row equals the number of garter stitch ridges needed for a perfect square. Geometry strikes again!

DESIGNING WITH SQUARES

One of the most striking aspects of working with mitered squares is the way that both color choice and placement can dramatically alter the look of a final piece. Similar to afghan squares or classic quilt design, arranging your squares in simple geometric patterns can create bold looks and striking effects. You can make an easy mitered square swatch with any yarn to test out your own patterns, and the individual practice squares could be used for coasters, washcloths, dolly blankets, or pieced together for an afghan. Try knitting your own following the instructions below, and then take a look at the color placements opposite for some inspiration. This is yet another example of a simple geometric technique that, when mastered, provides an easy route to endless experimentation and design opportunities.

MITERED SQUARE

Choose a needle that will produce a nice firm garter stitch fabric. Smooth yarns will show the stitches better.

1 Using long-tail method, CO an odd number of sts.

You need twice the number of stitches that you want the length of the edge of your square to be, plus one for the corner.

To set up: With the right side facing you, place a ring marker to the left of the three center stitches. You will slip the marker each time you encounter it. You may find after a while that you don't need to use the marker as you will be able to see where to make the decrease.

2 Row 1 AND ALL **WS** ROWS: K.

3 Row 2: K to marker, k3tog, k to end of row.

The cast-on tail will hang on the right edge of the right side.

4 Rep. rows 1–2 until 3 sts remain.

5 Cut the yarn, and knit 3 sts together pulling yarn through. Weave in ends.

Some people prefer a centered double decrease (see page 123). Try out both and see which you prefer.

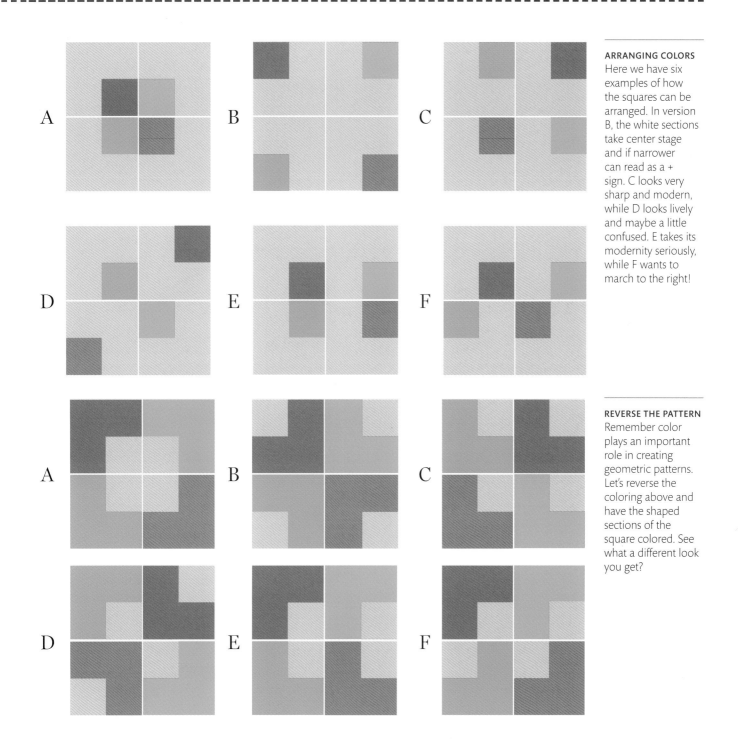

ARRANGING COLORS
Here we have six examples of how the squares can be arranged. In version B, the white sections take center stage and if narrower can read as a + sign. C looks very sharp and modern, while D looks lively and maybe a little confused. E takes its modernity seriously, while F wants to march to the right!

REVERSE THE PATTERN
Remember color plays an important role in creating geometric patterns. Let's reverse the coloring above and have the shaped sections of the square colored. See what a different look you get?

MITERED SQUARE PILLOW

This is a pillow that would be at home in the Paris apartment of Sonia Delaunay. The front of the pillow is made up of four small mitered squares, with one larger square for the back. Here you will make each square separately, but in the future, you might consider joining them as you knit (see page 66). The arrangement of the squares has been chosen already here, but you might like to make a different layout. There are lots of possibilities for a whole roomful of pillows!

BEFORE YOU BEGIN

PROJECT SPECS

FINISHED SIZE

14" x 14" (35.5 cm x 35.5 cm)

Each small square measures 7" x 7" (17.75 cm x 17.75 cm)

GAUGE

19 sts x 38 rows = 4" (10 cm) square in garter stitch

MATERIALS

YARN

Cascade Yarns 220 Superwash Aran, 100% Superwash Merino Wool, 3½ oz (100 g), 150 yds (137.5 m)

   Color A Black, 2 balls

   Color B Dark Aqua, 1 ball

   Color C Pumpkin, 1 ball

   Color D Jasmine Green, 1 ball

   Color E Magenta, 1 ball

NEEDLES

US 7 (4.5 mm) knitting needles or a 16" (40 cm) circular needle

NOTIONS

Stitch markers, tapestry needle, 16" (40 cm) pillow form

KEY TO YARN COLORS

Black

Dark Aqua

Pumpkin

Jasmine Green

Magenta

FRONT SQUARES

1 With color B, using long-tail method CO 65 sts.
Row 1 (AND ALL WS ROWS): Sl1, k to end of row.
Row 2: S1, k to marker, k3tog, k to end of row.

Set up: Place locking ring markers on each side of the three center stitches (stitches 32, 33 and 34). You will slip the markers each time you encounter them. You may find after a while you won't need to use them as you will be able to see where to make the decrease.

2 Work 17 ridges.
Cut color B and join color A.
Rep. rows 1–2 until 3 sts remain.

A ridge equals two rows in garter stitch.

3 Cut the yarn, and k3tog pulling yarn through. Weave in ends.

4 Work 3 more squares, following instructions as above.

Replace color B on the second square with color C, on the third square with color D, on the fourth square with color E.

BACK SQUARE

1 With color A using long tail method, cast on 129 sts.
Row 1 (AND ALL WS ROWS): Sl1, k to end of row.
Row 2: Sl1, k to marker, k3tog, k to end of row.

Set up: Place locking ring markers on each side of the center three stitches (stitches 64, 65, and 66).

2 Rep. rows 1–2 until 16 ridges have been worked.
Cut color A and join color B.

3 Rep. rows 1–2 until 11 ridges have been worked in color B.
Cut color B and join color C.

4 Rep. rows 1–2 until 11 ridges have been worked in color C.
Cut color C and join color D.

5 Rep. rows 1–2 until 11 ridges have been worked in color D.
Cut color D and join color E.

DOUBLE SIDED PILLOW
The design of this pillow works so that each side features a different pattern. Two stylish looks for your couch in one!

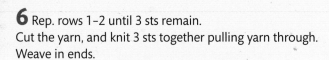

6 Rep. rows 1–2 until 3 sts remain.
Cut the yarn, and knit 3 sts together pulling yarn through.
Weave in ends.

When weaving in the ends, you don't have to be particular as they will be on the inside of the pillow.

FINISHING

1 Join the small squares together as shown in the image on page 65 (left), using mattress stitch to seam.

2 Seam three sides of the front to the back square, working from the outside.

Stuff the pillow case with a 16" (40 cm) square pillow form.

3 Seam shut with mattress stitch. Weave in ends.

DOMINO KNITTING

Just as dominoes are placed one after another in a game, in domino knitting pieces are joined together as the work progresses. If you want to try this for your cushion, it may be easier to use a circular needle, as the flexibility will help in the corners when picking up stitches. The directions for the first square would remain the same, but you would slip the first stitch in each row to make it easier to pick up stitches later. For the second square, you should begin with the new yarn in the corner that has just been completed, and pick and knit half the number of stitches in the original cast-on, including the corner stitch, which will be in the corner where you cast on the first square. Next, cast on the second half of the stitch count using the knitted cast-on method, and continue as before.

STOCKINETTE STITCH SQUARES

Decrease **stockinette stitch** at equal points to create versatile **squares**.

While mitered squares make fantastic pillows and afghans, stockinette stitch squares lend themselves more easily to wearable garments and accessories.

The simple squares of the Color Field Bags (shown left) are worked from the outside in by decreasing at four equidistant points. However, you could decrease at more points to create other shapes: five points for a pentagon, six for a hexagon, and so on. These shapes, that have squared outer edges, often become the basis of circles when knit because the fabric is soft and flexible. Hexagonal and octagonal shapes regularly form the tops of hats, the most striking being a Fair Isle tam, which showcases the decreases to form part of the pattern. Once you have mastered the basic square, you can try decreasing at more points to create a varied array of geometric shapes.

Using this decreasing technique to create shapes also allows for a creative use of color and proportion. While the rigid shapes of mitered squares utilize bold pattern repeats for graphic effects, the looser structure of decreased squares provide a canvas to try out interesting placements that pull the eye in or even trick it into seeing movement within static objects.

Inspiration!

Turn a Square by Jared Flood

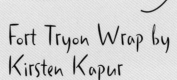

Fort Tryon Wrap by Kirsten Kapur

Strong squares can make striking fashion accessories and bold garment designs.

PROPORTION AND SCALE

To find inspiration for your square and color placement, start pondering the shapes of buildings when you are out and about. Is a construction two squares in height with a smaller square as the portico? How are the windows of a skyscraper stacked? When you begin to notice the geometric relationships in everyday things, you will develop your instincts as both a designer and a knitter.

Considering proportion and scale are of particular importance when working with squares. Two large squares in a pattern will have a different effect to many tightly packed squares, and focusing the center of the squares to one edge of your garment or item will also draw the eye up or down in interesting ways. Do you prefer equally spaced shapes, like the panes of a window, or seemingly random placements that play with your perception? Squares can look neat and precise or strikingly chaotic.

THE EFFECT OF COLOR

As well as the size and placement of your squares in relation to others, color plays an important role in the appearance of proportion. The way you use color can drastically change the effect a piece has, by altering not only its basic look, but the initial response it demands. Take for instance the two bags on page 73. In the small bag, the rich river blue deepens and seems to pull the center of the square in, while in the large bag the red center square pops out! This is because cool colors recede, while warm colors come forward. Many lessons of color theory can be explored just by knitting this bag with different colors.

A lot of people are afraid of working with color and believe they are just "not good" at color. The truth is that it takes experimentation and practice. Think of a project as a color experiment and take each new piece as a chance to expand and develop your knowledge and understanding. (For more information on how to choose color, see pages 110–113.)

ABOVE New Log Cabin Washcloths by Purl Soho
Notice how color placement radically changes the look of these two squares. The top square has a balance of color while the bottom arrangement draws the eye to the center.

OPPOSITE Get creative and experiment with different color combinations and patterns. See how the placement of warm and cool colors can create very different effects.

RAGLAN SHAPING

A modified version of the same shaping that you will tackle in the Color Field Bag, overleaf, is just how the yoke of a circularly knit, seamless raglan-sleeved garment is constructed. The body and sleeves are knit separately, then joined at the underarms where the yoke begins. To shape the yoke, decreases are made on each side of each sleeve join, decreasing quite rapidly (often every other round) to give a more curved shaping. When making the Color Field Bag you will want the finished piece to lie flat, so will be decreasing less often. Applying similar color bands to a raglan sweater would give a color block graphic effect at the yoke.

Lila Raglan Sweater by
Carrie Bostick Hoge

COLOR FIELD BAG

These bags both follow the same format, starting with a large number of stitches and decreasing until only four remain. Because the square is worked in stockinette stitch and it needs to lie flat, you will not decrease every other row, as you did with the even stitch-to-row ratio of garter stitch.

BEFORE YOU BEGIN

PROJECT SPECS

FINISHED SIZE

For small bag: 9" x 9" (23 cm x 23 cm) square.

For large bag: 11" x 11" (28 cm x 28 cm) square

GAUGE

10½ sts x 15½ rounds = 4" (10 cm) square in stockinette stitch, with yarn used doubled.

MATERIALS

YARN

Quince and Co Puffin, 100% American Wool, 3½ oz (100 g), 112 yds (102 m)

For small bag

Color A Kumlien's Gull, 1 ball

Color B Iceland, 1 ball

Color C River, 1 ball

For large bag

Color A Peak's Ferry, 1 ball

Color B Dogwood, 1 ball

Color C Malbec, 1 ball

Yarn used doubled.

NEEDLES

US 11 (8 mm) circular needle, 16" (40.5 cm) length

Double-pointed needles

NOTE ON SPECIAL STITCHES:

This pattern uses the centered double decrease (cdd) stitch. See page 123 for the instructions for this technique.

KEY TO SMALL BAG YARN COLORS

■ Kumlien's Gull

■ Iceland

■ River

KEY TO LARGE BAG YARN COLORS

■ Peak's Ferry

□ Dogwood

■ Malbec

MAKE TWO PANELS

For both the sizes you will need to make two panels to form the front and the back of the bag. You will seam the panels together in step 3 of the finishing instructions.

SMALL BAG (MAKE TWO SIDES)

1 With color A, holding two strands together, with long-tail method CO 84 sts.

Join for working in the round, being careful not to twist.

SET UP ROUND: * Pm, k 21 sts; rep from * 3 more times.

It's a good idea to make the first marker a different color than the others.

2 **ROUND 1 (DECREASE ROUND):** Sl marker, * k to 3 sts before next marker, cdd; remove marker, k1, replace marker; rep from * 3 more times. 76 sts.

ROUND 2: K (slipping all markers).

You will place the handle in the next round.

ROUND 3 (DECREASE ROUND): Rep. round 1. 68 sts. Handle: k4, BO 8 sts, k3, cdd.

Now you will complete the handle in this round.

ROUND 4 (DECREASE ROUND): Rep. round 1. 52 sts. k3, CO 8, k3, cdd.

Using cable method and working from the back, CO 8 sts. Turn work and resume as usual. 60 sts.

3 Join color B.
ROUND 5: K.
ROUND 6 (DECREASE ROUND): Rep. round 1. 52 sts.
ROUND 7 (DECREASE ROUND): Rep. round 1. 44 sts.

4 Join color C.
ROUND 8: K.

KNITTING WITH DOUBLED YARN

When planning to hold two strands together, wind the yarn into a center-pull ball and take one strand from the middle and the other from the outside.

Continue in the decrease pattern set. Here you will essentially be repeating rounds 1–8, but with fewer stitches between each cdd.

ROUND 9 (DECREASE ROUND): Rep. round 1. 36 sts.
ROUND 10: K.
ROUND 11 (DECREASE ROUND): Rep round 1. 28 sts.
ROUND 12 (DECREASE ROUND): Rep round 1. 20 sts.
ROUND 13: K.
ROUND 14 (DECREASE ROUND): Rep round 1. 12 sts.
ROUND 15 (DECREASE ROUND): Rep round 1. 4 sts.

FINISHING

1 Cut yarn, leaving a 4" (10 cm) tail, and weave in ends.

2 Wash and block both pieces to 9" (23 cm) square.

3 When dry, with color A and WS facing, seam.

With a tapestry needle, using mattress stitch seam three sides of the bag, leaving the edges with handles open.

LARGE BAG (MAKE TWO SIDES)

1 With color A, using two strands at once, with long-tail method CO 108 sts.

Join for working in the round, being careful not to twist.

SET UP ROUND: * Pm, k 27 sts; rep from * 3 more times.

It's a good idea to make the first marker a different color than the others.

2 **ROUND 1 (DECREASE ROUND):** Sl marker, * k to 3 sts before next marker, cdd; remove marker, k1, replace marker; rep from * 3 more times. 100 sts.

ROUND 2: K (slipping all markers).

ROUND 3 (DECREASE ROUND): Rep. round 1. 92 sts.

You will place the handle in the next round.

ROUND 4 (DECREASE ROUND): K5, BO 10, k4, cdd. Resume, working as for round 1, with cdd at each remaining corner. 84 sts.

3 Join color B.

You will complete the handle in this round.

ROUND 5 (DECREASE ROUND): K3, turn work, with WS facing and using cable method CO 10 sts.

Turn work. With WS facing again, k3, cdd.

Resume, working remaining two sides of square as for round 1, with cdd at each corner. 76 sts.

ROUND 6: K.
ROUND 7 (DECREASE ROUND): Rep. round 1. 68 sts.
ROUND 8: K (slipping all markers).
ROUND 9 (DECREASE ROUND): Rep. round 1. 60 sts.

4 Join color C.
RND 10 (DECREASE ROUND): Rep. round 1. 52 sts.
RND 11: K (slipping all markers).
RND 12 (DECREASE ROUND): Rep. round 1. 44 sts.
RND 13 (DECREASE ROUND): Rep. round 1. 36 sts.
RND 14: K.
RND 15 (DECREASE ROUND): Rep. round 1. 28 sts.
RND 16: K.
RND 17 (DECREASE ROUND): Rep. round 1. 20 sts.
RND 18 (DECREASE ROUND): Rep. round 1. 12 sts.
RND 19: K.
RND 20 (DECREASE ROUND): Rep. round 1. 4 sts.

FINISHING

1 Cut yarn, leaving a 4" (10 cm) tail, and weave in ends.

2 Wash and block both pieces to 11" (28 cm) square.

3 When dry, with color A and WS facing, seam.

With a tapestry needle, using mattress stitch seam three sides of the bag, leaving the edges with handles open.

GARTER STITCH AND STOCKINETTE CIRCLES

Start from the center and knit outward to make **stockinette stitch circles**, or begin at the edge and work your way in for **circles** made in **garter stitch**. Go big for rugs or take it small for coasters.

We see circles everywhere we look, in fashion, graphic design, industrial design, and home goods, and from rugs and cushions to round tables and windows. Traditional dwellings such as felt yurts or mud huts in Kutch, India are both based on a circular floor plan, as were ancient roundhouses, and on the runway, striking dot patterns and millinery styles celebrate the circle.

In knitting, circles form the basis of many lace shawl patterns, mind-blowing in their complexity. It is a method of shawl-making found in many parts of the knitting world. Based on simple geometry, circular shawls can be knit from the center out by doubling the number of stitches at regular intervals in one round. Elizabeth Zimmerman, the mother of modern knitting, nicknamed this construction the "Pi Shawl." Having the increases happen all at once, in evenly spaced concentric circles, allows for the insertion of many different lace stitches or simple color changes without as much planning or math needed as other circular shawl constructions, such as a spoked or spiral increase. It's a technique you'll find useful in your future knitting pursuits. This same circle construction can be taken and applied to other uses. Pillows, table mats—even a garment, with strategically placed armhole openings.

Inspiration!

Moon Pie by Susan Barstein

Urania's Tam by Romi Hill

Circles in all forms—large, small, radiating, dotty— feature regularly in fashion and interior collections.

KNITTING CIRCLES

There are several clever ways of shaping circles in hand knitting, whether starting from the inside out, or from the outside in. Knit circles can be made with garter stitch, stockinette stitch, or with complicated lace, and can quickly be transformed into any number of items. Obvious choices would be place mats, coasters, table-coverings, or shawls, but you could also sew two big circles together and attach handles to make a bag. Insert some concentric circles in a different color and you'd have a unique item with an op art, geometric look.

   Similarly to knit squares or crochet circles, making lots of small circles can also be a great way of putting together an afghan. Pick some ice-cream pastel shades in green, pink, yellow, and blue and pair with soft gray tones for a tasteful yo-yo baby afghan.

GARTER STITCH CIRCLES

On the next pages you will learn how to make a stunning stockinette stitch rug, but knowing how to create perfect circles in garter stitch will help you expand your horizons for other projects, too. Try this quick garter stitch circle, which decreases at six points every other round. You'll see that although they look like circles, they are actually hexagons. If you decreased at eight points instead, you would have made octagons. These little circles are used as coasters in my house, but they would also be perfect for sewing together for a knit afghan.

GARTER STITCH CIRCLE SWATCHES Knit simple circles in garter stitch or stockinette—go big for rugs and shawls or stay small and make yo-yo afghans and place mats.

DAISY MAT GARTER STITCH CIRCLES

Although you are actually making a hexagon, yarn is so pliant and flexible that the finished result will resemble a circle.

YARN

Berroco Ultra Alpaca, 52% Acrylic, 40% Wool, 8% Nylon, 3½ oz (100 g), 215 yds (198 m)

Color A Winter White

Color B Light Gray

NEEDLES

US 6 (4 mm) dpns

1 Using long-tail method, CO 48 sts.

Arrange 16 stitches on each of three double-pointed needles.

Join for working in the round, taking care not to twist.

2 ROUND 1: P.

Because you are working garter stitch in the round, every other round will be purled.

3 ROUND 2 (DECREASE ROUND): K6, k2tog, rep. to end of round. 42 sts.

You will be decreasing at 6 points on every decrease round, with one less stitch between decreases as the circle gets smaller.

4 Continue, alternating rounds.

ROUND 3: P.
ROUND 4: (DECREASE ROUND): K5, k2tog, rep to end of round. 36 sts.
ROUND 5: P.
ROUND 6 (DECREASE ROUND): K4, k2tog, rep to end of round. 30 sts.
ROUND 7: P.
ROUND 8: (DECREASE ROUND): K3, k2tog, rep to end of round. 24 sts.

ROUND 9: P.
ROUND 10 (DECREASE ROUND): K2, k2tog, rep to end of round. 18 sts.
ROUND 11: P.
ROUND 12 (DECREASE ROUND): K1, k2tog, rep to end of round. 12 sts.
ROUND 13: P.
ROUND 14 (DECREASE ROUND): K2tog, rep. to end of round. 6 sts.

5 Cut yarn and thread through 6 remaining sts. Weave in ends.

Make six white circles and one gray.

FINISHING

1 Sew flat edges together to form a daisy.

2 Wet block, teasing the outside edges of the petals into circles.

For a larger circle, cast on a greater number of stitches in a multiple of six (try 60 for a good size coaster or 120 for a tea pot mat.)

Project

SUPER CHUNKY STOCKINETTE STITCH CIRCLE RUG

This rug is influenced by Elizabeth Zimmerman's Pi Shawl which sprung from the mathematical principal of pi (π), whereby the circumference of a circle measures π times the circle's diameter. For this project, it means starting at the center and doubling the stitches at regular intervals to create an ever-expanding circle that lies flat. Yarn overs are the increase of choice here, and whether you know it or not, this is your first foray into lace knitting! The rug is finished with several rows of garter stitch to firmly frame it.

BEFORE YOU BEGIN

PROJECT SPECS

FINISHED SIZE

27" (68.5 cm) diameter

GAUGE

Blocked: 6 sts x 8 rounds = 4" (10 cm) square in stockinette stitch

MATERIALS

YARN

Wool and the Gang Crazy Sexy Wool, 100% Wool, 7oz (200 g), 87 yds (80 m)

    Color A Big Bird Yellow, 2 balls

    Color B Sand Trooper Beige, 1 ball

NEEDLES

US 17 (12.75 mm) dpns

US 17 (12.75 mm) circular needle, 32" (81 cm) length

US 17 (12.75 mm) circular needle, 24" (60 cm) length

Optional: US 17 (12.75 mm) circular needle, 32" (81 cm) length

NOTIONS

Stitch marker, tapestry needle, T-Pins for blocking

Optional: Locking ring marker

KEY TO YARN COLORS

Big Bird Yellow

Sand Trooper Beige

1 With color A and dpns, using the backward loop method CO 6 sts.

Place stitch marker and join for working in the round. At this point I use three needles with two stitches on each. For a marker I use a length of looped and knotted yarn in a thinner weight and different color than my main color, as I find it does not fall off the end of the points like a plastic marker might. I also like to place a locking ring marker in the first stitch to indicate the start of a round and move it up as the work progresses, but this is entirely up to you.

2 ROUND 1 (INCREASE ROUND): *K1, yo; rep from * 6 times. 12 sts.

This round will double the number of stitches. The following rounds will be plain knitting.

3 ROUNDS 2–4: K.

For most of the knitting your work will look like a bag or a giant hat, but rest assured that once off the needles it will become a flat circle.

4 ROUND 5 (INCREASE ROUND): *K1, yo; rep. from * 12 times. 24 sts.

The number of plain rounds before increase rounds is getting larger, providing areas where a small lace pattern could be inserted.

5 ROUNDS 6–11: K.

At this point I find the stitches get crowded, so you can try rearranging the stitches over four needles, with six stitches on each.

TRY THIS FIRST

The beginning of this rug is a bit fussy. I suggest making a small sample version as described in the swatches on page 79. Using smaller needles and thinner yarn may allow you to get the hang of things more easily. On the other hand, the large needles might work best for you. Everyone is different so choose which method you prefer, and remember this start is awkward for everyone when trying it for the first time.

6 ROUND 12 (INCREASE ROUND): *K1, yo; rep. from * 24 times. 48 sts (12 on each needle).

The stitches may have become crowded again, so here you can try moving them onto a circular needle. Just begin knitting with the new needle to transfer the stitches. Make sure your stitch marker that indicates the beginning of the round is in place.

7 ROUNDS 13–18: K.

8 ROUND 19 (INCREASE ROUND: *K1, yo; rep. from * 48 times. 96 sts.

9 ROUNDS 20–25: K.

Cut color A, leaving an 8" (20 cm) tail.

THE BORDER

1 Join color B.

ROUND 26 (INCREASE ROUND): *K1, yo; rep. from * 96 times. 192 sts.

Try to keep the stitches fairly loose so they easily slide around the needle. It might be fiddly at this point because there are lots of stitches crowded on the needle. If you've invested in the long circular needle, I would use it now. If you choose to continue with a smaller circular needle, be careful. Though they seem indestructible because they are so hefty, needles are easily broken at this point. There is nothing worse than to have the cable snap off when you're moving 192 stitches, and to have them fall off and get loose.

2 Continue by alternating k and p rounds.
ROUND 27: K.
ROUND 28: P.
ROUND 29: K.
ROUND 30: P.

3 Bind off all stitches. Cut yarn, leaving an 8" (20 cm) tail.

FINISHING

1 Using tapestry needle, carefully weave in ends.

DRESSMAKER'S TIP: Bulky yarn can be difficult to thread onto your tapestry needle. Use the dressmaker's trick of folding the yarn across the needle lightly, and slide off, putting this folded edge through the eye of the needle.

2 Block carefully.

Blocking is an important step in circular construction. When you first slip it off the needles, your piece will look like a ruffly curiosity. It needs strict discipline to get into the proper shape. See page 137 for detailed instructions on how to wet block circular items.

STRANDED COLORWORK DOTS

Stack **dots**, vary their sizes, or play with color choice for a contemporary look.

You have seen how knitted circles can work for bold geometric items such as bags, rugs, and afghans. Now you can discover circles as a pattern on the surface of a fabric—dots!

Dots are found on all kinds of woven and knit fabrics. A look through the pages of folk costume and fashion history books reveal dots as a constant feature. Strangely, polka dots were named for the dance, not the polka costume, but they are a regular feature of Spanish flamenco costumes. Dots are also the main component in the life work of Japanese artist Yayoi Kusama who has used dots in many innovative and striking ways. Dots have a lot of character and inject an infectiously cheery mood into any piece, but they can also suggest an element of chaos and confusion, depending on their placement and numbers.

Different effects can be produced by playing with dots, varying their size and color and changing the distance between them. More modern dot patterns often have varying sizes of polka dots in the same piece.

Color can also dramatically change the appearance of a dotted fabric—you will be working stranded knitting, so the dots can only change color on different rounds, but you can easily change the colors in the middle of a dot, or use variegated yarn for a lively effect. Dots lend a graphic pop to knitted items, and the variations that can be achieved by simply staggering or stacking positions will keep you engaged and interested in trying out new arrangements. It is eminently pleasing to discover what can be done with the most elemental geometric shapes.

Inspiration!

Lichen Mitts by Mary Jane Mucklestone
Image by Carrie Bostick Hoge

Dots Cowl by Hilary Smith Callis

Dots are a constant favorite in fashion, always looking cheerful and happy.

DESIGNING WITH DOTS

Studying charts is a helpful way to understand the relationship between pattern elements. The charts on these pages are simple dot repeats, but by adjusting the sizes of the dots, the placement, and the color, different effects can be achieved.

The first chart shows dots placed equidistant apart with two stitches between each dot and two rows between each staggered dot, in a neat pattern. If we brought them closer they would still be dots, but depending on the colors chosen, the negative space will begin to show up becoming the dominant focus, giving a net-like effect. Enlarging the dots can eliminate this tendency, but this honeycomb effect can be used to an advantage when designing your own knits.

WEAVING FLOATS

The stranded colorwork projects in this book keep to the basic rules of traditional Fair Isle knitting. Most importantly, this means that the patterns are designed so that the floats on the reverse side of the fabric are never so long as to need special handling. As you continue in your colorwork pursuits, you may encounter stitch patterns that require you to carry the yarn not in use a fairly long distance before you use it again. To prevent strands catching on fingers and distorting the stitches, floats should be no longer than one inch. If a float needs to span a wider distance, it is best to "weave," "trap," or "tack"—all words that mean catching the float with the working yarn to keep it snug against the back of the work. This technique should be saved until you are comfortable with basic stranded knitting technique. See pages 126–127 for more information.

IMPERFECT CIRCLES

In stranded knitting you'll notice by looking at the charts that the edges of the dots are not smooth. They don't even really look like circles. If we could knit only half of a stitch then we might succeed in knitting perfect dots, but we can't, so we do our best. Though the dots don't really look circular on the chart, or even when you first begin to knit them, viewed from a distance they quickly begin to look the way they should.

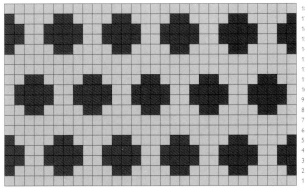

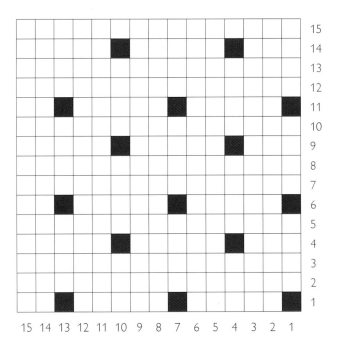

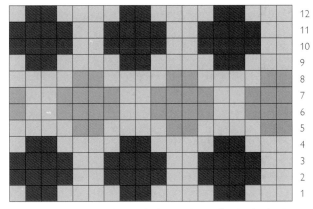

ABOVE The smallest motif of all, a single stitch, visually reads as a dot. It is one of the most common patterns of all!

ABOVE RIGHT The chart for the Dotted Mitts (pages 88–91) has equidistant dots. Up close the dot pattern almost looks like a chunky cross symbol, but once knit, they form cute and easy dots.

MIDDLE RIGHT Dots are actually made up of a chunky cross shape. Here they are placed closer than on the Dotted Mitts on page 88.

BELOW RIGHT Different sizes of dots create interest.

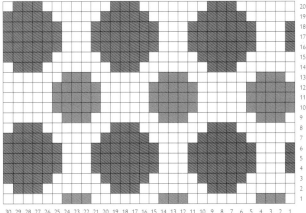

DOTTED MITTS

These mitts feature equidistant dots—up close the pattern almost looks like a chunky + symbol, but once knit, they form cute and easy dots.

BEFORE YOU BEGIN

PROJECT SPECS

Small (medium, large) : 6⅝ (8, 9)" [17 (20, 23) cm] circumference

GAUGE

11 sts x 11 rounds = 2" (5 cm) square in colorwork pattern using larger needles

MATERIALS

YARN

Berroco Ultra Alpaca, 50% Super Fine Alpaca, 50% Peruvian Wool, 3.5 oz (100 g), 215 yds (198 m)

For gray mitts

Color A Melon Mix, 1 ball

Color B Light Gray, 1 ball

Color C Grapefruit Mix, 1 ball

For blue mitts

Color A Grapefruit Mix, 1 ball

Color B Zephyr, 1 ball

Color C Winter White, 1 ball

NEEDLES

US 8 (5 mm) dpns

US 10 (6 mm) dpns

NOTIONS

Stitch marker, tapestry needle

KEY TO YARN COLORS

- ▨ Zephyr
- ☐ Winter White
- ▨ Grapefruit Mix

KEY TO YARN COLORS

- ☐ Melon Mix
- ▨ Light Gray
- ▨ Grapefruit Mix

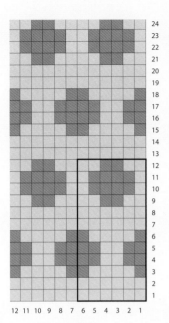

CHART FOR DOTTED MITTS Sometimes when you see a chart it is hard to make out what the design actually is, because it will often start in the middle, as in this dot chart. The large chart above has 24 rounds—the number of rounds needed to complete the stranded colorwork pattern for our mitts. The black box outlines the actual pattern repeat, which is a 6 stitch, 12 round repeat—the same as the chart below.

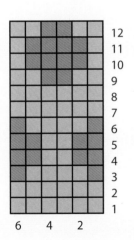

CHART COLOR KEY

■ Grapefruit Mix

▨ Light Gray

1 With smaller needles and color A, using long-tail method CO 32 (36, 42) sts.

Distribute the stitches onto three needles. Join for working in the round. Place marker to show the beginning of the round (a locking marker is good here, so that it doesn't fall off the end of the needle, and you can move it up as you progress).

2 K1, p1 rib for 2" (2.5 cm).

3 INCREASE ROUND: Keeping in rib pattern, increase 4 (6, 6) sts evenly around. *Work 8 (6, 7) sts, m1R, rep. from *. 36 (42, 48) sts.

I used a lifted increase, but you can use any increase you like. Rearrange the stitches so you have 12 (14, 16) stitches on each needle. Change to larger needles.

4 Work rounds 1–6 of colorwork chart, working 6 stitch repeat 6 (7,9) times.

Strand color not in use smoothly behind work.

5 ROUNDS 7–8

These steps will be worked with color B only, as rows 7 and 8 of the chart use only gray or blue yarn.

ROUND 7: BO the first 8 (8, 10) sts of round. Work to end of round.
ROUND 8: With backward loop method, CO 8 (8, 10) sts onto RH needle. Work to end of round.

6 Work rounds 9–12 of chart.

Continue following 12-round chart 3 times more.

7 With color B, k 2 rounds. With color A, k 1 round.

8 Change to smaller needles. Work 1" (2.5 cm) k1, p1 rib.

Bind off in rib.

THUMB

1 With a smaller needle and color A, pick up and k 8 (8, 10) sts from CO edge of thumb hole.

2 With another smaller needle, k 4 (4, 5) sts from CO edge.

USING DOUBLE-POINTED NEEDLES

Using double-pointed needles can seem awkward at first, especially when you are working with stranded knitting. Sometimes practicing on plain knitting is easier. See page 125 for more information.

This mitt pattern could be also be worked with stockinette stitch stripes in the round. Abandon the stranded pattern and simply stripe! I suggest stripes at least four rounds high. Just remember that when knitting stripes in the round you'll have a slight jog in the pattern where the last round meets the first. I challenge you to embrace the jog!

3 With another smaller needle pick up 4 (4, 5) sts from CO edge. You now have 16 (16, 20) sts on the needles.

4 Join for working in the round.

K 1, p 1 rib for 5 rounds.

Bind off in rib.

FINISHING

1 With tapestry needle, carefully weave in ends.

Take special care in the corners where the thumb joins the body of the mitt.

2 Block.

Carefully shape mitts into right hand and left hand and dry flat.

SECOND MITT

Make one more mitt. The mitts are interchangeable.

CHEVRONS

Chevrons offer a great canvas for experimentation, both in size and color.

Chevrons can be bold and blocky like vintage Marimekko shifts, or subtle and changing like the signature chevrons from Italian fashion house Missoni. In fact, the iconic status of Rosita and Ottavio Missoni's designs are a testament to the lasting impact of geometric patterns. They created a much-copied but never equaled look that combines zigzags, waves, and chevrons, and from this Missoni established a huge label and family business, with their chevron items popular even today.

You saw before how re-arranging diagonal stripes in stranded knitting can produce chevrons. All different chevron designs can be made this way, but there are a couple of things to be wary of. Firstly, you must be careful with very wide chevrons as the floats can become long, and secondly you must remember that there are limits to the number of colors you can use in stranded knitting while still having the pattern produce a clear chevron shape.

However, there is another way to make chevrons in knitting that is even easier and allows for lots of experimentation. Simply increasing and decreasing at regular intervals will make ordinary stripes turn into zigzag chevrons. It can be done in plain garter stitch and stockinette stitch alike—even lace can be constructed in this manner.

Inspiration!

Muckle Mitts by Mary Jane Mucklestone

Knitted Thistle Necklace by Amy Lawrence Designs
Image by Holly Booth

Bold chevron patterns are always a striking look whether on fashion accessories or garments.

KNITTING CHEVRONS

Carefully placed decreases can form a bias fabric to make squares, and the same technique can be used to make these easy chevrons, too. The Chevron Leg Warmers on the next pages will be made in stockinette stitch, to lessen the connection with afghans, which are most often constructed from garter stitch.

Chevrons made as a bias fabric are a really great place to experiment with color, because you can use as many as you like in a single piece. Variegated yarns can make zigzag stripes with very little effort. The choice of yarn can greatly change the finished piece—tiny delicate yarns can create feathery baby afghans or gossamer scarves, while a chunky yarn could form the backbone of a rug. Try wrapping yarns around a card to vary the width of the stripes used in a piece and try out colors to decide which you like best, or knit up swatches like these to practice the technique.

ZIGZAG EDGES

The cast-on and cast-off edge of a bias-knit chevron fabric will naturally come to points, with a zigzag edge. For the leg warmers in this lesson (see pages 97–99), the pattern begins with a generous stretch of ribbing to camouflage this trait. However, in future projects you could use this to your advantage. The points look wonderfully graphic at both ends of a table runner, and chevron lace makes lovely café-style curtains, with the pointed ends ideal for attaching hanging rings and the bottom border lending an element of interest. My personal favorite, however, is a long chevron scarf with small multicolored pom-poms attached to the points.

IRREGULAR STRIPE CHEVRONS

Different widths and colors of stripes lend different effects. Knit this swatch and notice how spacing the increases one stitch apart makes the "peaks" of the chevron pattern rounded, while the valleys remain sharp. Let yourself begin thinking about other ways to riff on this versatile pattern.

YARN

Berroco Vintage, 52% Acrylic, 40% Wool, 8% Nylon, 3½ oz (100 g), 217 yds (198 m)

Color A Orange

Color B Magenta

Color C Violetta

NEEDLES

US 7 (4.5 mm) knitting needles

1 Using long-tail method, CO 35 sts.

Row 1 (RS): K2, ssk, * k2, kfb, k1, kfb, k2, cdd; rep from * once more, k2, kfb, k1, kfb, k2, k2tog, k2.
Row 2 (WS): K2, p to last 2 sts, k2.

2 You can follow the row pattern that I did, or make up your own.

Rows 1–4: Color A.
Rows 5–6: Color B.
Rows 7–8: Color A.
Rows 9–14: Color B.
Row 15: Color A.
Rows 16–19: Color C.
Rows 20–40: Work color sequence in reverse.

3 Bind off. Weave in ends.

4 Wet block.

Take care to keep the selvedge edges straight. Pin the "peaks" and "valleys" to form lovely points.

IRREGULAR STRIPE CHEVRON SWATCH Knit with different widths and colors to achieve a range of effects for your chevron patterns.

OPPOSITE, FAR LEFT Spectrum by Joji Locatelli, image by Rafael Delceggio

VARIEGATED YARN CHEVRONS

Use a variegated yarn to add color and interest to chevron patterns with little fuss. In this swatch we are using m1R and m1L with one stitch between to form a very sharp peak without the little "bar" that kfb produces, resulting in a more subtle shaping.

YARN

Molly Girl Rockstar, 100% Superwash Merino, 215 yds (197 m)

NEEDLES

US 7 (4.5 mm) knitting needles

1 Using long-tail method, CO 35 sts.

Row 1 (RS): K2, ssk, * k3, m1R, k1, m1L, k3, cdd; rep from * once more: k3, m1R, k1, m1L, k3, k2tog, k2.
Row 2 (WS): K2, p to last 2 sts, k2.

2 Bind off. Weave in ends.

VARIEGATED YARN CHEVRON SWATCH
Variegated yarn is a fun and simple way to add interest to chevron patterns.

Project

CHEVRON LEG WARMERS

These graphic retro leg warmers are a simple yet satisfying project. They could be made in gentle neutral shades of soft wool, or bold rainbow hues for children.

BEFORE YOU BEGIN

PROJECT SPECS

FINISHED SIZE

S (M, L): 12 (15, 17)" (30.5 [38, 43] cm) circumference, 16¼" (42 cm) tall

GAUGE

19 sts x 24 rows = 4" (10 cm) square in stockinette stitch

MATERIALS

YARN

Cascade Yarns 220 Superwash Aran, 100% Superwash Merino Wool, 3½ oz (100 g), 150 yds (137.5 m)

  Color A Black, 2 balls

  Color B White, 1 ball

NEEDLES

US 7 (4.5 mm) dpns

NOTIONS

Locking stitch marker, tapestry needle

KEY TO YARN COLORS

□ White

■ Black

LEANING INCREASES

This pattern uses a quick and easy increase, kfb. It is sometimes called a "bar increase" because it makes a little bar like a purl bump. It is a fast and furious increase requiring minimal thought and action. You could choose to knit pairs of left-leaning and right-leaning increases, which are less visible and a little more elegant. In that case, round two would read as follows:

ROUND 2 (AND EVERY EVEN ROUND): *M1R, k6 (8, 9), cdd, k6 (8, 9), m1L; rep. from * 4 times.

INCREASES AND DECREASES

On every other round, you will be increasing on each end of every needle and making a centered double decrease in the middle.

1 With color A, using long-tail method CO 60 (76, 84) sts.

Divide the stitches evenly over four needles, 15 (19, 21) stitches on each, and join without twisting for working in the round. Place locking ring marker to indicate beginning of the round.

K1, p1 rib for 4" (10 cm).
K 1 round.

2 With color B begin chevron pattern.
ROUND 1 (AND EVERY ODD ROUND): K.
ROUND 2 (AND EVERY EVEN ROUND): *Kfb, k5 (7, 8), cdd, k5 (7, 8), kfb; rep. from * 4 times.
Rep. rounds 1–2.

3 With color A, work rounds 1–2 twice.

4 Continue as above, alternating 4 rounds color B and 4 rounds color A 6 times.

5 K1, p1 rib for 4" (10 cm).

Bind off.

FINISHING

1 Weave in ends.

2 Block.

JOINING NEW COLORS

You can choose to cut the yarn each time you change colors, leaving a 4" (10 cm) tail and carefully weaving in the ends when finished. This will help eliminate the slight jog created by knitting in the round when a new color is introduced. Because these are leg warmers, they are easy to wear with the join on the inside of the leg where it will not be very noticeable. If you are careful, you can even keep the yarn attached and bring the yarn not in use up, eliminating the need to cut the yarn, and thus, creating a vertical float. Take care not to pull too tight, which could cause bunching.

MIX UP YOUR SHAPES!

Experiment, persevere, and enjoy bold **shapes**, colors, and knits!

We've explored a lot of fun geometric concepts in this book, discovering clever ways of shaping and introducing colors into our knitting projects. You can take it to another level by combining some of the things you've learned. Take inspiration from the images on this page, try creating your own colorwork chart, or simply add a new shape into one of the earlier project patterns, making a completely new piece! Remember, you can mix things up by combining shaped pieces, or by including different motifs into stranded colorwork. You could arrange small individually-made shaped circles into various geometric patterns, sew them all together and edge with squares. Or, include corrugated ribbing (see page 39) at the beginning of a project for a flash of vertical stripes. That being said, stranded colorwork is perhaps the easiest method for mixing up shapes. Take a look at the chart opposite to see how simple it is to include different shapes in one piece.

In this Icelandic Lopapeysay, square shapes combine with half circles and vertical stripes to form a motif reminiscent of peacock feathers.

ABOVE Stopover by Mary Jane Mucklestone. Photograph © Kathy Cadigan

LEFT Modern Colorwork Cowl by Mary Jane Mucklestone. Photograph © Craftsy

44 43 42 41 40 39 38 37 36 35 34 33 32 31 30 29 28 27 26 25 24 23 22 21 20 19 18 17 16 15 14 13 12 11 10 9 8 7 6 5 4 3 2 1

30 29 28 27 26 25 24 23 22 21 20 19 18 17 16 15 14 13 12 11 10 9 8 7 6 5 4 3 2 1

TRIANGLE STRIPE SCARF

Try combining the garter stitch stripes from Lesson One with garter stitch triangles from Lesson Four. Start knitting triangles as per the instructions for afghan squares or pennants, but keep knitting wider until you have the width you would like the scarf to be, maybe 45 stitches total. At this point, don't begin decreasing, but continue on in garter stitch, including stripes whenever you feel like it. Continue for as long as you like, remembering that garter stitch will grow in length when worn. Finish by decreasing to a point—you'll have a cute scarf with points at each end. Attach a pom-pom or tassel to the ends!

MULTI-SHAPE HAT

Make a hat that combines the triangles from the first chart in Lesson Five, and finish it with plain stockinette stripes at the top. Because you will be knitting circularly, the plain stripes will not match up exactly, but with a fine yarn this won't be noticeable.

___

MULTI-SHAPE HAT
A fun beanie hat is a great canvas for mixing different shapes.

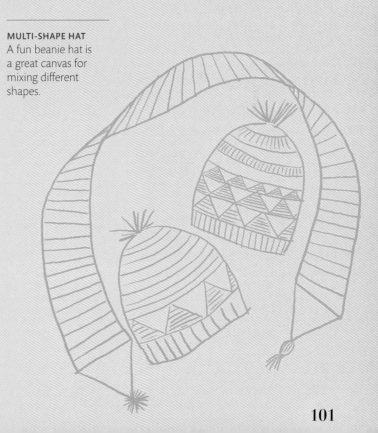

Try alternating segments of the diagonal stripes pattern of Lesson Two with the dot chart from Lesson Nine.

ABOVE Machine knitted cushions by Seven Gauge Studios, Knitted Spot Cushion and Geo Cushion Image by Studio Photography Carmel King

CHAPTER 2
BASIC TECHNIQUES

Knitting is a personal art and every knitter has their preferred methods that seem to fit them best, but first you will need to try out the different techniques available and practice your skills. These pages will teach you some of the most important knitting techniques that you will need to knit the projects in this book.

CHOOSING YOUR TOOLS

There are many tools out there designed for knitting. You can go wild and get every latest thing, but it basically boils down to two essentials: sticks and string!

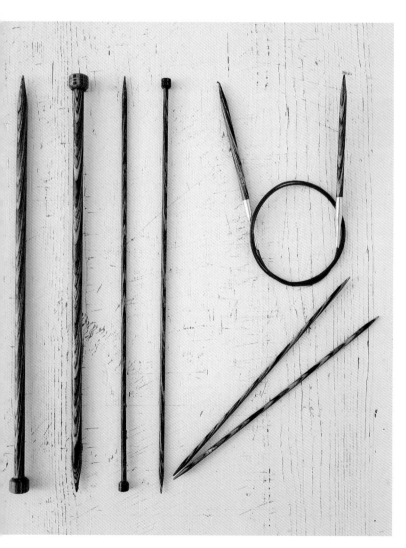

NEEDLES

It is worth investing in good needles since you will use them for years. Bamboo or metal is a matter of personal choice. For circular needles, it is essential to get needles with a smooth join between cable and needle.

NEEDLES You will need straight, circular, and double-pointed needles; the latter two for working in the round.

DIAMETERS Needles come in different diameters so that the knitted stitch achieves the correct gauge for the article being made.

LENGTHS The length of the needle depends on the amount of stitches needed for an item. For straight knitting, shorter lengths are used for dishcloths, baby clothes, and narrow scarves, while longer needles are used for adult garments. In circular knitting, the needle length must be shorter than the circumference of your work. 24–32" (60–80 cm) circular needle lengths are customary for sweaters, 16" (40 cm) for hats, and double-pointed needles for sleeves, mittens, socks, and the tops of hats.

LEFT Straight needles, circular needles, and double-pointed needles. Circular needles consist of two needle tips separated by a length of flexible cord, while double-pointed needles are used in sets of four or five. Experiment with what works best for your project.

HELPFUL FOR KEEPING YOUR PLACE ON THE CHART

- Post-it notes—my favorite!
- Magnetic ruler—some people swear by them
- Clear plastic ruler—another handy item

NOTIONS

Although all you really need are needles and yarn, these little extra accessories help to make your projects go much smoother and are nice to have in your notions bag. I always like to choose beautiful gadgets that I will treasure for years.

NEEDLE GAUGE Very helpful and handy, as not all needles are marked with a size and they can look frustratingly similar. A needle gauge has a series of holes to indicate size. Try the holes until you find the one nearest to your needle's diameter.

STITCH MARKERS Stitch markers come in a variety of styles and you will want to try them all. Bright plastic rings close in size to your needle are very helpful for marking off stitch repeats. Use a different color to indicate the beginning of the round. Locking stitch markers are useful for making vertical notations, such as counting rows or rounds. They are also useful to mark the beginning of the round when using double-pointed needles, where the ring markers would slide off, and to indicate the front of your work.

SCISSORS AND TAPE MEASURE Small, sharp scissors or snips are indispensable. Small dressmaker-type tape measures should be marked with both inches and centimeters.

TAPESTRY NEEDLE Essential equipment for weaving in ends and grafting stitches. They are available in plastic or metal. The bent ended ones are my favorite.

STITCH HOLDERS Double-ended stitch holders are great for holding shoulder stitches—you can even knit or graft right off them.

ROW COUNTER A row counter is helpful for keeping track of rows, provided you remember to click it!

PINS T-Pins or long pins with cute flowered tops are needed for pinning garments in place while blocking flat, and for aligning seams when joining your work with mattress stitch.

PENCIL AND A SMALL NOTEBOOK Pencils are always handy for making notations on patterns, ticking off rows, and jotting down adjustments. A notebook is useful for making note of new ideas and inspirations. Ones with graph paper are especially nice for making up your own pattern motifs.

BALLOONS Great for blocking hats.

POM-POM MAKERS For fashioning perfectly spherical pom-poms.

CHOOSING YARN

Choosing the right yarn is essential for the success of your projects. You want to use yarn you like and that will work well for the project. On top of this, other factors may influence your selection, such as the climate of where you live and the cost of the yarn.

TYPES OF YARN

The first thing you should know when selecting yarn is its fiber content—what raw materials are used in making up the yarns. It can be natural, made from materials such as cotton, wool, linen, alpaca, or other specialty fibers. Or, it can be man-made from natural plant products, such as rayon or acetate. Yarn can also be synthetic, made from petroleum products such as polyester, nylon, acrylic, or spandex.

Wool from sheep is the quintessential fiber for hand knitting. It is strong, insulating, and has a bouncy resilience especially prized in knitwear. The less processed wools still contain some lanolin making them somewhat water repellent. There are many different breeds of sheep and each has its own special qualities. Explore your local yarn shops to discover wool treasures.

YARN SUBSTITUTION

Sometimes you may need to substitute the yarn used in a project. It could be unavailable in your area, discontinued, or you might just want to use yarn from your stash. Whatever the reason, there are several things you'll want to consider.

YARN Experiment with different yarn types and colors to find one that works best for your project.

NATURAL ANIMAL FIBERS	NATURAL PLANT FIBERS	NATURAL INSECT FIBERS	MAN-MADE CELLULOSE-BASED FIBERS	MAN-MADE SYNTHETIC FIBERS
Wool from sheep. Exotic animal fibers like musk ox, yak, cashmere goats, vicuña, alpaca, and rabbit.	Spun from cotton, hemp, flax, or bamboo.	Silk from silkworms.	Man-made materials made from natural plant products, such as rayon, viscose, and acetate.	Made from synthetic polymers, such as acrylic, nylon, and polyester.

Can you get the gauge called for in the pattern? You can get a general idea by checking the ball band of the yarn to see what the manufacturer's suggested gauge is, but the only way you will know for sure is by knitting a swatch in the stitch pattern called for in the pattern, then washing and blocking that swatch. See page 114 for more information on gauge.

Does the yarn have the same properties of the yarn called for in the pattern? Different yarns behave differently. Alpaca will drape, while pure cotton may stretch under its own weight. Analyze the picture of the garment you're intending to knit for other clues. Is it a cardigan knit in the round with steek stitches at the front that will later be cut? If so, you will need a traditional, minimally-processed yarn for the best results.

How much yardage will you need? You'll need to match the yardage given. It is wise to have extra in the event the yarn behaves differently than you anticipate!

DECIPHERING THE BALL BAND

Different producers will give varying amounts of information.

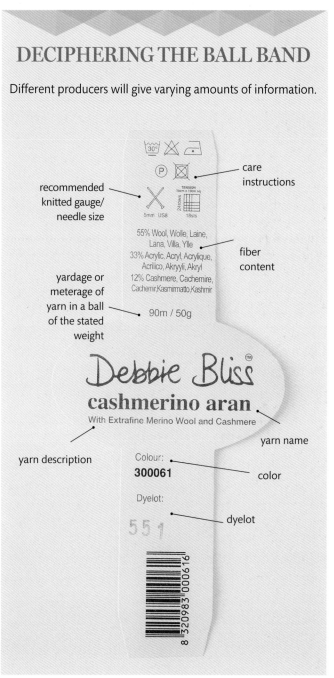

recommended knitted gauge/ needle size

care instructions

55% Wool, Wolle, Laine, Lana, Villa, Ylle
33% Acrylic, Acryl, Acrylique, Acrilico, Akryyli, Akryl
12% Cashmere, Cachemire, Cachemir,Kasmimatto,Kashmir

fiber content

yardage or meterage of yarn in a ball of the stated weight

90m / 50g

Debbie Bliss ™

cashmerino aran

With Extrafine Merino Wool and Cashmere

yarn name

yarn description

Colour: **300061**

color

Dyelot:

551

dyelot

YARN WEIGHTS

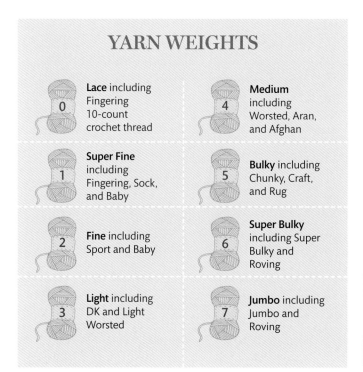

0 — **Lace** including Fingering 10-count crochet thread

1 — **Super Fine** including Fingering, Sock, and Baby

2 — **Fine** including Sport and Baby

3 — **Light** including DK and Light Worsted

4 — **Medium** including Worsted, Aran, and Afghan

5 — **Bulky** including Chunky, Craft, and Rug

6 — **Super Bulky** including Super Bulky and Roving

7 — **Jumbo** including Jumbo and Roving

HOLDING THE YARN

There are many, many different ways of holding the yarn when knitting and all of them are the "right" way as long as you are happy with your result and it is not causing any physical pain. Try several different methods to find out which way works for you.

There are two major ways of holding the yarn, either in the left hand (often called "continental"), or in the right hand (sometimes called "English," "throwing," or even "American style"). The two methods shown below illustrate how the yarn may be wrapped around the fingers of either the left or right hand. There are many variations on this and you should never feel it is wrong to either wrap the yarn more than once around a finger or to weave the yarn through the fingers.

HOLDING THE NEEDLES There are many different ways to hold knitting needles, including the continental style shown above. Find the method that is most comfortable for you.

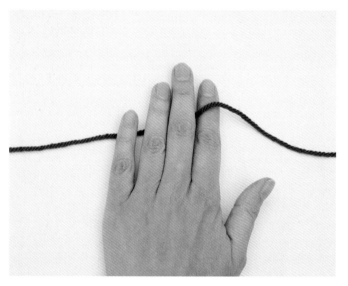

HOLDING YARN, LOOSE HOLD To hold the yarn loosely, hold the yarn in the palm of your hand and loop it over your forefinger. For right-handed knitting wrap the yarn through the fingers of the right hand in the same way.

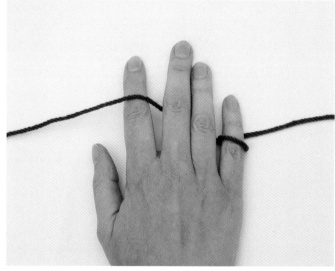

HOLDING YARN, FIRM HOLD To hold the yarn firmly, wrap the yarn around the little finger and then around the forefinger. For left-handed knitting, wrap the yarn through the fingers of the left hand in the same way.

HOW TO CHOOSE COLOR

Having fun with color is one of the reasons I'm so drawn to knitting. I love to see the ball of luscious color transformed by patient stitching into something useful and beautiful. Some knitters are timid when they approach color, not believing they have the ability to choose the right colors or combinations. Nonsense! It is just a matter of learning to see color and understanding a few things about color relationships.

It is helpful to look at the color wheel to remind yourself how colors are arranged on the spectrum. Simply identifying colors and their relationship to one another trains your eyes to really study them. The basics of color theory are useful, to build a common language to describe colors and their attributes. It's both fun and educational to study the color wheel.

HUE
The first word to know is hue, which is simply the name for a pure color such as red, blue, or green. Navy is not a hue—navy is a shade of blue.

PRIMARY COLORS
First, find the primary colors red, blue, and yellow that are equally spaced around the wheel. In theory, all colors are made by mixtures of these three.

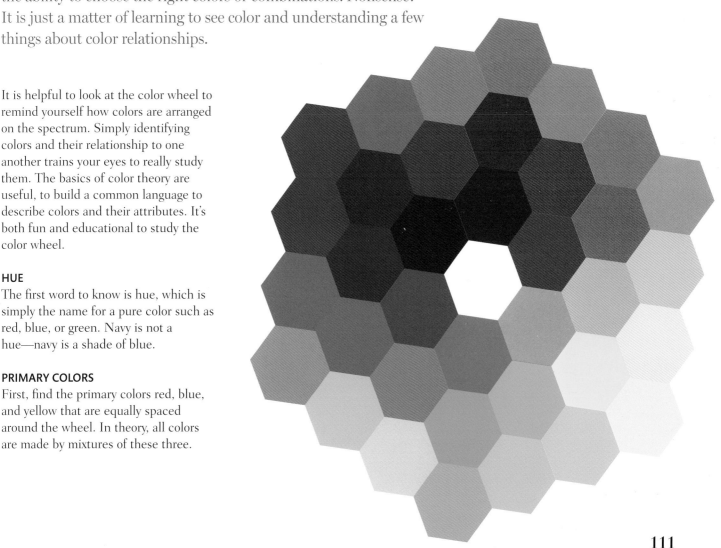

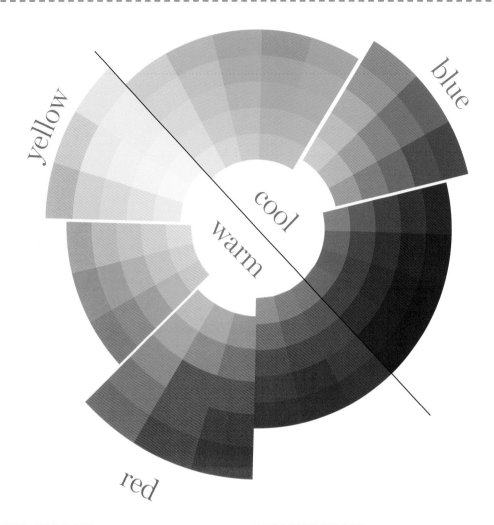

SECONDARY AND TERTIARY COLORS

Mix two primary colors and you will get a secondary color. Red plus yellow equals orange. Add a little more red and you will have red-orange, a tertiary color. Add a little more yellow and you will have yellow-orange, another tertiary color. This mixing goes on around the wheel.

COMPLEMENTARY COLORS

Colors directly across the wheel from one another are called complementary colors—blue and orange, for example. Used in combination, they are typically vibrant and sometimes shocking! Complementary colors can work well as accents.

ANALOGOUS COLORS

Colors that lie next to one another are called analogous colors. They're almost sure to be a pleasing combination. They are often found in nature, and are comfortable and harmonious.

WARM COLORS AND COOL COLORS

We can bisect the color wheel into warm colors and cool colors. Cool colors often seem to recede, while warm colors appear to come forward.

TINTS, TONES, AND SHADES

But what about the other colors like browns or pastel colors? Why aren't they on the color wheel? There are other terms for these—tints, tones, and shades. Color theory was initially developed for painting, which involved mixing colors to find the exact effect desired. When you add white to a hue, you get a tint. When you add gray to a hue you get a tone. Adding black makes a shade.

We're talking about fiber, though. I like to think of the fleece of a sheep—one in natural white and another dyed red. Imagine carding a little of the white fleece into the red. The more you add, the lighter the fleece will get, and eventually it will begin to appear pink, which is a tint of red. The same could be done with a gray fleece or a black fleece. Adding gray to the dyed red fleece makes tones of red, while adding black makes different shades of red.

VALUE

Perhaps the most important thing to think about with yarns, especially when knitting stranded colorwork items, is value—the lightness or darkness of a color.

It is good practice to get accustomed to seeing colors in terms of value rather than just "color." For instance, a gray scale is a group of grays that range from white to black. Attempting to arrange your yarns like this, in a sequence from light to dark, can be challenging. It may be hard to decide the best positions, but I urge you to try, as it is a useful exercise in understanding value. One popular trick is to take a black and white photograph of your yarns. The resulting photo can give you a good indication of value. Be warned however, your eye is a better judge than the camera lens. Saturated colors (very bright colors, like those of printing ink in cyan blue, magenta and yellow) do not appear in black and white as they do in real life—they trick the camera! Let your own eyes be the final judge. Believe it or not, squinting can help.

SWAPPING OUT COLOR

All the projects in this book use fairly bright and cheery colors. Imagine them worked in only natural sheep colors, producing a lovely, yet completely different effect! Sketch your design and try out a few different color combinations, keeping in mind the different properties that each color will bring. When using two colors in the same round, you want to make sure there is enough difference in value for the pattern colors to show up against the background colors. The more you play with color, the more you will begin to understand how it works.

GAUGE

Before starting a project, you will need to knit a swatch to measure your gauge. The gauge is the number of stitches and rows (or rounds) in a 4-inch (10-centimeter) square. You'll need to know your gauge both when following written patterns or when designing. In the first case, to make sure the garment will come out to the desired size, and in the second, to calculate the number of stitches and rounds needed for your design.

Since you want your gauge swatch to approximate your actual knitting, you must use the method called for in the pattern. If the project is worked back and forth in rows, the swatch should be worked in rows. Likewise, if the project is worked in the round, the swatch should be knitted in the round as well.

Begin by using the needle called for in the pattern and cast on enough stitches for a generous 4" by 4" (10 cm by 10 cm) swatch. I suggest casting on enough stitches for at least a 6" (15 cm) square, so you have a decent square to measure, not affected by the edges of the swatch, which may be distorted. Follow the stitch pattern exactly, knitting until you have a square piece. It is important to wash and block your swatch to get a true representation of the finished fabric. Wash the swatch as you would your finished garment and dry flat.

MEASURING YOUR GAUGE

To measure stitches, place the dry piece on a flat surface. Lay a ruler or stitch gauge across the stitches and pin on each side of 4" (10 cm). Count the number of stitches. If the number of

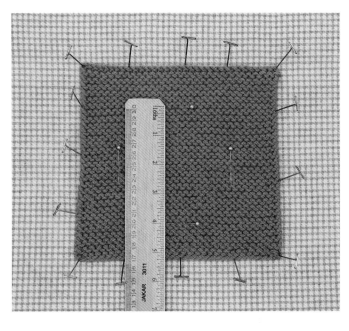

LEFT Use pins to secure your gauge swatch to the board before measuring with a ruler or stitch gauge.

stitches is too few, you are knitting at a looser gauge than the pattern calls for. You can try going down a needle size. If you have too many stitches, your gauge is tighter than the pattern calls for. You can try going up a needle size.

To measure rows, lay the ruler up and down along the rows of stitches, placing pins on each side of 4" (10 cm). Count the number of rows. If the marked rows

are too few, your piece will be shorter than the pattern calls for, and if there are too many, it will be longer. Try different needle sizes, or make adjustments to the pattern to accommodate the differences. Of the two measurements, stitch gauge is most important. It is easier to adjustment garment length than circumference.

HOW TO READ CHARTS

Pattern motifs for stranded knitting are charted on graphs. Each square represents a single stitch and every horizontal row of squares indicates a row or round of the pattern repeat. When there are several pattern motifs in the garment, there will often be one chart with as many stitches represented as the largest pattern motif. The smaller motifs will be repeated for that number of stitches. At other times, there will be several charts—one chart for each individual pattern motif.

The chart is read just as your knitting will be worked. When knitting circularly, read the chart from right to left, and from bottom to top. Circular knitting charts are numbered up the right side, indicating the round number. Most charts for stranded knitting are written for working in the round. Charts written specifically for knitting back and forth in rows are numbered on both sides, with odd numbers on the right side, and even numbers on the left. When working flat, you will read every odd numbered row from right to left, knitting every stitch on the front of the work. Even numbered rows will be read from left to right, purling every stitch, across the wrong side of the work.

READ YOUR KNITTING

Learn to "read" your work as well as the chart; really look at what you've knit and watch the pattern emerge from the background. A nice trick is to place a Post-it note over the rows you've worked, leaving the row just worked uncovered so that you can still see the stitch you are working into. By reading your work you'll see where you've been, and by consulting the chart, see where you'll be going.

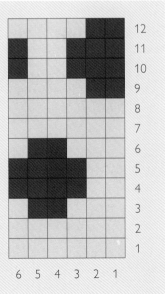

ABBREVIATIONS

Though they may look daunting at first glance you will soon become familiar with the format of knitting patterns. You can always refresh your memory using the list of standard abbreviations below.

* repeat directions between * as many times as indicated

BO bind off

CO cast on

CDD centered double decrease

DPNS double-pointed needles

K knit

K2TOG knit next two stitches together as one

K3TOG knit next three stitches together as one

KFB knit into front and then back of stitch

M1 make one

M1L make a left-leaning stitch

M1R make a right-leaning stitch

P purl

PM place marker

REP repeat

RS right side

SL slip next stitch onto the right-hand needle without knitting or purling

SSK slip first stitch and then 2nd stitch knitwise, insert left needle into stitches and knit next two stitches together as one

ST(S) stitch(es)

YO yarn over

TOG together

WS wrong side

CASTING ON

Before you start knitting, you need to cast on stitches. There are many ways to cast on and the method you choose will depend on what you are trying to achieve. You might need a tough edge, or a flexible edge, for example. You'll also find that some cast-ons work better for you than others, so experiment with what you find easiest.

SLIPKNOT

Use a slipknot to put the first stitch on the needle.

1 Lay the yarn on a flat surface and make a circle about 6" (15 cm) from the end.

2 With your fingers or needle tip, reach through the center of the circle and pull a loop of the working yarn through the center. If you used your fingers, place this loop on the needle.

3 Now gently pull both the tail and the working yarn below the needle. Tighten by pulling on the working yarn.

1

2

3
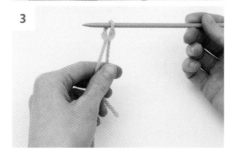

KNIT CAST-ON

The knit cast-on is easy to execute and makes a nice corded edge.

1

2

3

4

1 Place a slipknot on your left needle.

2 Put your right needle through the loop as if to knit.

3 Pull the stitch through.

4 Place the stitch back on left-hand needle. You now have two stitches on the left-hand needle.

5 Repeat steps 2–4 for the desired number of stitches.

LONG-TAIL CAST-ON

This is my favorite cast on, because once you know how to do it, it is fast and easy. There is one downside—you have to estimate the amount of yarn you'll use before you start. I wrap the yarn around my needle 20 times, and then measure the length. Then I use that measurement to calculate how much yarn I will use for each 20 stitches I'll be casting on, plus a little extra for good measure.

Set up Measure out the amount of tail you'll need for the cast-on as detailed above, and make a slipknot here.
1 Place slipknot on your right needle.
2 Make a "V" shape with your left thumb and left index finger, with your palm facing you.
3 With the tail end in front, wrap the tail end around your left thumb, back to front, and the working yarn (ball end) around your left index finger, front to back. Grasp both ends with curled fingers.
4 Bring the needle up through the loop around your thumb.
5 Take the needle over the top of the yarn around the forefinger and draw the yarn around the forefinger through the loop under the thumb, at the same time, dropping the yarn off your thumb and tightening the loop around the needle.
6 Replace the tail yarn on your thumb and repeat steps 4–6.

BACKWARD LOOP CAST-ON

1 Place a slipknot on your right needle, leaving a 6" (15 cm) tail.
2 Wrap the yarn around your left thumb counterclockwise and grasp the end with the curled fingers in the palm of your hand.
3 Insert the needle under the front of the yarn and gently tighten the loop while slipping it onto the needle.
4 Repeat steps 1–3 for the desired number of stitches.

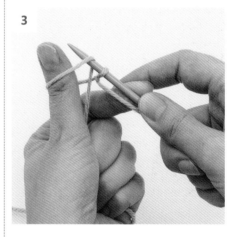

With practice you will be able to make this cast-on in two smooth movements.

BASIC STITCHES

The most elemental techniques of all knitting are the knit stitch and the purl stitch. Essentially, purling is like backwards knitting. Once you have mastered knit and purl, you are halfway to making almost anything you would like!

KNIT STITCH

Hold the yarn and needles whichever way you prefer.
1 Insert the right-hand needle into the first stitch on the left-hand needle, from the left to the right.
2 Wrap the yarn under the tip and then over the right-hand needle and draw the yarn through the stitch.
3 Slip the stitch off the left-hand needle and onto the right-hand needle.

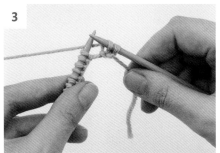

PURL STITCH

Hold the yarn and needles whatever way you prefer.

1 Bring the working yarn to the front.
2 Insert the right-hand needle into the first stitch on the left-hand needle, from right to left in the front.
3 Bring the yarn in front of the right-hand needle, wrap the yarn over the needle and draw the yarn through the stitch.
4 Slip the stitch off the left-hand needle and onto the right-hand needle.

STOCKINETTE AND GARTER STITCH

In this book, you will use stockinette and garter stitch to create most items. Garter stitch is the most basic knitting. It is made by knitting every stitch on every row, or knitting and purling alternate rounds. This creates a lovely ridged, squishy fabric that doesn't curl.

Stockinette stitch combines knit and purl, alternating every row, or knitting every round. Stockinette makes a smooth fabric with lots of little "V"s on the front of the fabric. It will curl at the edges.

STOCKINETTE STITCH

GARTER STITCH

SEED STITCH

You may also come across seed stitch in your knitting pursuits. In this technique, a textured fabric is created by alternating knit and purl stitches both horizontally and vertically. To do this, you will knit in the purl stitches of the previous row, and purl in the knit stitches.

WORKING WITH TWO COLORS

When you have two colors working at the same time, sometimes you will want to carry the yarn not in use carefully up the side of the work.

1 Catch the yarn on every other row on the right side.
2 Pick up the working yarn on the right side, under the yarn being carried.
3 When a new yarn is introduced, drop the old yarn in front and pick up the new yarn from behind.

RIB STITCH

To knit rib stitch, you will switch between knit and purl stitches in the same row. This creates vertical columns of knit and purl and creates a stretchy fabric that is ideal for hugging the body. The simplest ribbing is 1x1 (single rib) or 2x2 (double rib), but there are many different variations.

To knit k1, p1 (1x1) ribbing in rows or rounds, you will need to cast on the number of stitches specified and knit one then purl one stitch to the end of the row or round, ending with either a knit or purl stitch. On the next row or round, knit into knit stitches and purl into purl stitches.

To knit k2, p2 (2x2) ribbing, you will knit two stitches before purling two, in the same way.

SHAPING

Knitters can shape their work as they go by using decreases to make the fabric narrower and increases to make it wider. Strategic placement of single decreases and increases will allow your knitting to form geometric shapes such as triangles, squares, and circles. The same techniques can be applied to garments, where increases and decreases are used to shape sleeves, armholes, necklines, and waist shaping.

INCREASES

There are so many different ways of increasing—the most important thing is just to find your own favorite method. Sometimes, a knitting pattern won't tell you which type of increase to use, instead simply instructing you to "make one". That's when all this practice comes in handy!

KNIT FRONT AND BACK, OR BAR INCREASE (KFB)

This is perhaps the easiest increase. It makes a little bar at the base of the new stitch, making it easy to see (and therefore to count) between rows with shaping.

1 Knit into the front of the stitch on the left-hand needle and pull the loop through but leave the stitch on needle.
2 Knit into the back of the same stitch on the left-hand needle.
3 Slip the stitch off the left-hand needle, making two stitches on the right-hand needle.

1

2

3

LIFTED INCREASES

This type of increase is made by working into the strand between the stitches. It is nearly invisible. Depending upon which way you lift the stitch, it will either lean to the left or to the right.

LEFT-LEANING LIFTED INCREASE (M1L)

1 Use the tip of the right-hand needle to pick up the strand between the stitches on the needles, from back to front.
2 Place the tip of the left-hand needle through the front of this lifted stitch and knit into the back of it with the right-hand needle, sliding the stitch onto the right-hand needle.

1

2

RIGHT-LEANING LIFTED INCREASE (M1R)

1 Use the tip of the left-hand needle to pick up the strand between the stitches on the needles, from back to front.
2 With the right-hand needle, knit into the front of this lifted stitch, sliding the stitch to the right-hand needle.

1

2

BACKWARD LOOP INCREASES

These increases use the same motion as the backward loop cast on, and much like m1R and m1L, they can be left leaning and right leaning.

BACKWARD LOOP INCREASE, RIGHT LEANING

1 Using the fingers of your left hand, twist the working yarn counterclockwise to form a small loop with the ball end of the yarn on the front of the loop, and place on the right-hand needle.

BACKWARD LOOP INCREASE, LEFT LEANING

1 Using the fingers of your left hand, twist the working yarn clockwise to form a small loop with the ball end of the yarn at the back of the loop, and place on the right-hand needle.

DECORATIVE YARN OVER INCREASE

This is a beautiful, airy increase that is used in lace knitting stitches. This increase is often paired with a decrease stitch so the work remains the same width.

YARN OVER INCREASE

1 Bring the working yarn to the front and knit the next stitch in the normal way. This leaves an extra loop, with the new stitch on the right-hand needle.
2 When you next encounter the stitch, work as you normally would.

DECREASES

Decreases are used wherever you want a garment to get smaller, like shaping the crown of a hat, waist shaping, or a neckline in a circularly knit yoke. Sometimes decreases can be decorative, leaning left or leaning right.

KNIT TWO TOGETHER, RIGHT-LEANING SINGLE DECREASE (K2TOG)

1 Work to the position of the decrease.
2 Insert the right-hand needle through the front of the first two stitches on the left-hand needle.
3 With the tip of the right-hand needle, catch the working yarn and pull a loop back through both stitches, off the left-hand needle and onto the right-hand needle.
4 Two stitches have become one, slanting right.

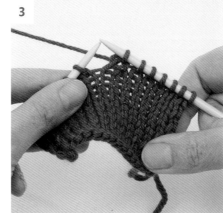

PRINCESS LINE SHAPING

Work a right-leaning decrease near the beginning of the row and a left-leaning decrease at the same point near the end of the row. Likewise, use the same slanting pairs when increasing. When worked closer to the center of a garment, this shaping is called "Princess Line Shaping."

SLIP SLIP KNIT, LEFT-LEANING DECREASE (SSK)

1 Work to the position of the decrease.
2 Slip the first stitch on the left-hand needle knitwise onto the right-hand needle.
3 Slip the next stitch on the left-hand needle knitwise onto the right-hand needle.
4 Bring the left-hand needle through the front of these two stitches on the right-hand needle and knit together.
5 Two stitches have become one, slanting left.

BALANCED SINGLE DECREASES

Choosing the best decrease for the stitch pattern is essential for shaping garments. Working single decreases in pairs can produce elegant decorative effects, which are often an element of lace stitch patterning as well as armhole and neckline shaping.

DOUBLE DECREASE (K3TOG)

1 Work to the position of the decrease.
2 Insert the right-hand needle through the front of the first three stitches on the left-hand needle.
3 With the tip of the right-hand needle, catch the working yarn and pull a loop back through all three stitches, off the left-hand needle and onto the right-hand needle.
4 Three stitches have become one.

CENTERED DOUBLE DECREASE (CDD)

1 Work to one stitch before position of the decrease.
2 Slip two stitches onto the right-hand needle together, as if to knit.
3 Knit the next stitch on the left-hand needle.
4 Pass both slipped stitches over the just knitted stitch.

LEFT A centered double decrease is used in the Chevron Leg Warmers (see pages 97–99).

CIRCULAR KNITTING

Circular knitting, or knitting "in the round," is a way of knitting that creates a tube of fabric without seams. Circular knitting uses circular or double-pointed needles, and is begun by joining the cast-on edge—care must be taken not to twist the cast-on edge round the cable, as this will cause your knitting to twist and take on a figure eight shape. Twisting at the beginning cannot be rectified later—you would have to rip out your work and start again. Double-pointed needles are used when a piece of knitting is too small in diameter for circular needles. In circular knitting, the right side or outside of the fabric is always facing the knitter.

CIRCULAR NEEDLES

1 Cast on the total number of stitches, and lay the needle on a flat surface with the cast-on edge on the inside. The stitches should be arranged evenly on the needle.

2 Pick up the needles, so that the tips point toward you and the working yarn is on the right, with the yarn attached to the ball hanging outside of the circle.

3 Place a marker for the beginning of the round, making sure the cast-on edge is not twisted. To join, use the needle tip in the right hand to work the stitches on the needle tip in the left hand. Continue knitting as usual, pushing the stitches up the left needle, and smoothing out the just-knit stitches along the right-hand needle.

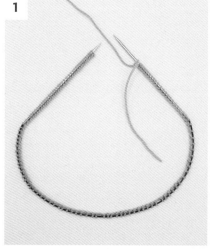

1

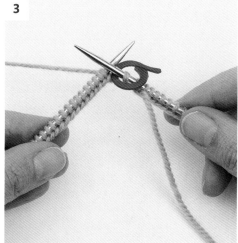

3

DOUBLE-POINTED NEEDLES

1 Cast on the total number of stitches onto one needle, then carefully transfer the stitches to two or three other needles, as close to the same number of stitches on each as possible.

2 Arrange the needles in a triangle, with the cast-on edge in the center of the triangle. Make sure the cast-on edge is not twisted.

3 Bring the first and last needles together and use the spare needle to knit with. As a needle becomes free, use it to knit the stitches from the next needle.

2

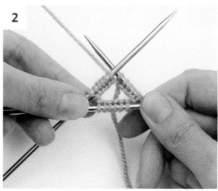

3

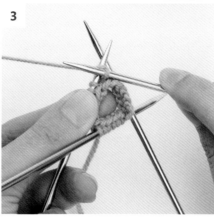

1

LEFT Double-pointed needles are used for making small circumference items such as socks, sleeves, or mittens.

MAGIC LOOP

There are other clever methods you might research for circular knitting small circumference items, such as using two circular needles, or manipulating a very long circular needle for the "magic loop" technique. Rather than use the entire cable, you pull out a small loop and divide your stitches between that and the needle tips. This method might be used for projects such as the mitts in Lesson Nine (see pages 88–91).

STRANDED COLORWORK

Once you get the hang of knitting with one color, you will probably want to try your hand at stranded knitting—knitting patterns by using two colors in the same round. It is often referred to as Fair Isle knitting, but that is a very particular type of stranded knitting. In all kinds of stranded knitting, as you knit with one color, the yarn not in use is carried across the back of the work, creating strands called floats.

HOLDING THE YARNS

There are numerous ways to hold the two colors of yarn in stranded knitting. One color in each hand or both colors in the left hand are most common. Try both and find which way is most comfortable for you. Try to keep your fingers close to the needles to help you control the tension.

YARN DOMINANCE

In stranded knitting, it is useful to think of the yarns as either the pattern color or the background color. While you knit, one yarn will appear slightly more dominant— either the pattern color or the background color. Yarn dominance occurs because one strand travels across the back of the fabric lower than the other, causing a slightly larger stitch. This is the dominant yarn. The yarn traveling in the higher position on the back of the work creates a slightly smaller stitch. The yarn held furthest to the left, no matter what way you hold your yarn, is usually the dominant one. Most often we want the pattern color to be dominant, and therefore it will be held in the position most to the left, while the background will be held to the right. Remember, however, that everyone is different. You should knit a swatch to find out which of the two positions is the dominant yarn for you. The most important thing is to be consistent in holding your yarn—assign one position for the pattern color and one for the background color and keep them in the same position while knitting your entire piece.

MANAGING FLOATS

While stranding, make sure that the floats do not become too short, causing a puckered fabric. As you knit, smooth your work out along the right-hand needle, so the yarn not in use will strand along behind the just-knitted stitches and automatically be the correct length. Floats that are too long are less of a problem, but they can make the stitches too tall, making your work look uneven.

MAAKIN' BELT

On Fair Isle and other Shetland islands, the maakin' belt, or knitting belt, is employed in combination with a set of 14" (35 cm) steel double-pointed needles. It is a cushion made of leather, stuffed with horsehair, pierced with small holes and worn on a belt around the waist. One end of a knitting "pin" is inserted in one of the small holes. This helps support the knitting, acting as a "third hand," allowing the knitter (with practice) to achieve great speed, as well as mobility. Old-time knitters often knit throughout the day while doing other tasks, such as hauling peat home for the fires.

JOINING NEW YARNS

When joining a new yarn, whether in stranded colorwork or when making a new color stripe, there is nothing special or fancy that you need to do, simply begin knitting with the new yarn, leaving a 2-4" (5-7 cm) tail. You will weave in this tail during the finishing . If you are changing colors a lot, you may want to stop periodically and weave the ends in, to lessen the amount of finishing you'll need to do at the end of your project.

BINDING OFF

Also called casting off, binding off links the final stitches of a piece to make a tidy edge that will not unravel. Although there is a basic method, like most techniques there are many variations to explore.

BASIC KNIT BIND-OFF

1 Knit two stitches as usual.
2 Insert the tip of the left-hand needle into the stitch furthest from the tip on the right-hand needle and lift over the last stitch you knit, off over the tip of the right-hand needle.
3 Knit one more stitch, and continue this way until one stitch remains.
4 Cut the yarn, leaving a 6" (15 cm) tail, and draw the end through the last stitch.

2

3

PURL BIND-OFF

1 Purl two stitches as usual.
2 Insert the tip of the left-hand needle into the stitch furthest from the tip on the right-hand needle and lift over the last stitch you purled, off over the tip of the right-hand needle.
3 Purl one more stitch, and continue this way until one stitch remains.
4 Cut the yarn, leaving a 6" (15 cm) tail, and draw the end through the last stitch.

2

BIND-OFF IN RIB
Bind off stitches as they appear in your rib pattern.

FOR A K1, P1 RIB PATTERN
1 Knit the first stitch.
2 Purl the second stitch.
3 Insert the tip of the left-hand needle into the stitch furthest from the tip on the right-hand needle and lift over the last stitch you purled, off over the tip of the right-hand needle.
4 Work one more stitch in the pattern set and continue to pass the stitch furthest from the tip on the right-hand needle over the first.
5 Repeat step 4 to the end of the row or round. Cut the yarn leaving a 6" (15 cm) tail and draw the end through the last stitch.

FOR A K2, P2 RIB PATTERN
1 Knit two stitches as usual.
2 Insert the tip of the left-hand needle into the stitch furthest from the tip on the right-hand needle and lift over the last stitch you knit, off over the tip of the right-hand needle.
3 Purl the next stitch.
4 Insert the tip of the left-hand needle into the stitch furthest from the tip on the right-hand needle and lift over the last stitch you purled, off over the tip of the right-hand needle.
5 Purl the next stitch.
6 Insert the tip of the left-hand needle into the stitch furthest from the tip on the right-hand needle and lift over the last stitch you purled, off over the tip of the right-hand needle.

7 Work one more stitch in the pattern set and continue to pass the stitch furthest from the tip on the right-hand needle over the first.
8 Repeat step 7 to the end of the row or round. Cut the yarn leaving a 6" (15 cm) tail and draw the end through the last stitch.

THREE-NEEDLE BIND-OFF
This bind-off is useful for joining two pieces of live knitting, eliminating the need for a sewn seam. It is used in the tablet case on page 40. The two pieces must have the same number of stitches.
1 Hold the two needles with the stitches to be joined, with the tips pointing right and with the right sides of the fabric facing each other.
2 With a third needle, knit together a stitch from the front needle with one from the back needle.
3 Repeat step 2.
4 Pass the stitch furthest from the tip on the right-hand needle over the second stitch as in a regular bind off.
5 Continue knitting a front and back pair of stitches and then binding off until all the stitches have been joined and bound off.

CHAPTER 3
FINISHING TECHNIQUES

Some people are daunted by the tasks required for finishing knitting projects. I say, embrace the finishing! Consider it a totally different thing from your knitting—a separate, skilled set of tasks that require thought and precision. By all means don't rush it. Don't spoil all your hard work with hasty or sloppy finishing.

SEAMING

I used to loath seaming, but now I find it one of the most satisfying of all tasks. Seaming is often done with the yarn you used for the project. In some cases, especially if the yarn is loosely spun, it is safer to use a slightly finer, stronger plied yarn in a similar color. Before seaming, analyze where you will be making the seam. You will be catching the horizontal "bars" between the first and second stitch columns on both sides, going from one side to the other side, and into the same stitches twice.

SEAMING STOCKINETTE STITCH TO STOCKINETTE STITCH (MATTRESS STITCH)

1 With the right-sides facing you, lay the two pieces on a flat surface with the edges to be sewn next to each other and the cast-on edge facing you. You may want to place some pins to line up rows, especially if you are attempting to match stripes.

2 With a tapestry needle threaded with your seaming yarn, insert the needle from front to back between the first and second stitches on the first row of the left-hand piece, pull the yarn through leaving a 4" (10 cm) tail.

3 Insert the needle into the right-hand piece, from front to back between the first and second stitches, and pull the yarn through.

4 Return to the left-hand side and insert the needle from the right side to the wrong side in the same place, where the yarn previously came out of the fabric. Slip the needle up to the horizontal bar in the row above and through to the right side.

5 Cross to the other side and repeat step 4.

6 Repeat steps 4–5 until the seam is complete, pulling the work tightly together every four or five stitches.

7 Make a loop at the end and thread the tail through. Pull tight to knot. Weave in the end.

5a

5b

6

SEAMING GARTER STITCH TO GARTER STITCH

1 With the right sides facing you, pick up the "bump" that protrudes from the selvedge, which is actually the center of the ridge.

2 Pick up the corresponding bump on the opposite selvedge.

3 Repeat steps 1–2. Every few rows, tighten the seam and the garter ridges will line up nicely.

LEAVE A TAIL

If you know you'll be seaming an edge, leave an extra long tail at the end of your bind-off to seam with. You'll have a secure beginning and one less tail to weave in.

WEAVING IN ENDS

Once your knitting is complete you will need to weave in all the loose ends. There are several different methods you can try for a tidy finish.

IN GARTER STITCH

Duplicate stitching into the ridges is the easiest way to weave in ends in garter stitch. Follow the course of the stitching from one ridge to the other, catching the purl bumps.

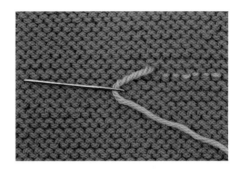

WHERE COLORS ARE JOINED IN KNITTING

From the back, lay the old color tail to the right and weave in that direction. Lay the new color tail to the left and weave in that direction. Either follow the course of the stitches in a duplicate stitch or catch the purl bumps for about an inch. Cut the tail ends to ½" (1.5 cm).

IN RIBBING

From the back, use the tip of a tapestry needle to catch ½ stitch in a vertical row of knit stitches for about an inch, or through the entire length of the ribbing. Pull the yarn through, and cut leaving a ½" tail (1.5 cm).

TROUBLESHOOTING

If you find a mistake in your knitting you'll want to stop and correct it. If it is a few stitches back, you can quite easily undo the work stitch-by-stitch. If the mistake is rows back, it is easier to take the work off the needles and rip back to just before the offending stitch. In both cases, you'll want to mark the place with a safety pin or locking ring marker.

UNDOING STITCH-BY-STITCH

1 Place a safety pin or locking ring marker on the mistake.
2 Working in the opposite direction as your knitting, place the point of the empty needle through the stitch below the last stitch on the other needle, from the direction that the stitch was pulled through.
3 As you place the lower stitch on the empty needle, gently pull the newer stitch out.
4 Repeat until you reach the mistake.
5 Resume knitting correctly!

RIPPING OUT ROWS

1 Place a safety pin or locking ring marker on the mistake.
2 Slide your needle out of the stitches.
3 Pull gently on the working yarn, undoing the stitches until you reach the row above the mistake.
4 Place your work so that the working yarn is on the right.
5 Insert the tip of your needle into the row below, and gently pull to undo the stitch above.
6 Continue until you reach the mistake.

SPIT-SPLICING

On some occasions you will want to avoid having tails to weave in, for instance on a reversible piece where it may show. Or, you might run out of yarn in the middle of a row and want to avoid undoing your work back to an edge. If you have a non-superwash wool you may be able to spit-splice your yarns, creating a nearly invisible join. Like all things, it takes a bit of practice. This method will not work with synthetics or superwash yarns.

1 Take the two ends of yarn you wish to join and separate the plies a bit.
2 Place the yarns in the palm of your hand, overlapping the ends of the yarn by a couple of inches, with the frayed ends intermingling.
3 Spit onto them (or dribble some water onto them, but spit works better!)
4 Rub the yarn between your two palms until the ends felt.

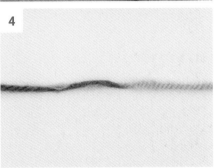

BLOCKING

Proper finishing is essential for all knitting. This means gently washing and carefully blocking your items. Most, if not all, irregularities in your knitting will magically disappear. The knitting will smooth out, eliminating any surface bumps, and the garment itself will relax and soften. Blocking should be done before you seam garments together and then again once seamed.

WET BLOCKING

1 Wash your knitting in tepid water with a mild soap, squeezing gently, not agitating.

2 Rinse thoroughly in water of the same temperature. Press gently against the sides of the basin to squeeze out excess moisture, then roll up in an absorbent towel and press down to get even more moisture out. Your damp garment will be surprisingly flexible and ready to grow into the shape you assign it!

3 Lay your knitting on a flat surface, such as a bed or a rug covered with towels. A blocking board is also not difficult to make—just a piece of plywood with one side covered with several layers of quilter's batting and then covered with a piece of checked fabric to assist in garment placement.

4 Gently push the knitting into the correct shape, using your measuring tape for correct sizing and pin placement.

5 Pin into place.

6 Let dry.

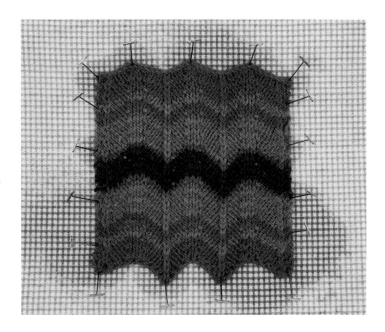

STORING KNITWEAR

Make sure to store your knits flat, carefully folded. If they are to be put away for the winter, fold them with tissue paper, to lessen the creases. To discourage moths, slip in a piece of cedar.

Don't be stingy with pins while blocking!

BLOCKING CIRCULAR PIECES

Circular pieces such as the rug on page 80 might need some specific thought when blocking. Not only do you want to get a nice, even circular shape, they can also be large and cumbersome. Be careful when blocking large pieces or items that need to be a particular shape, as they can be awkward and heavy and liable to stretch in alarming ways!

1 Wash your knitting in tepid water with a mild soap, squeezing gently, and not agitating.
2 Rinse thoroughly in water of the same temperature. Press gently against the sides of the basin (or bathtub) to squeeze out excess moisture.
3 Spread the item out on a flat surface (I use a rug covered with a large towel for big pieces), and moving your hands from the center out, encourage it to flatten out into a perfect circle.
4 Then, take a string attached to a pin at the center of the item and make a knot at half the diameter of the finished piece. Move the pin around in a circle like the hand of a clock, making sure the outer edge lines up with the knot. Pin at four points first (12, 3, 6, and 9 on a clock) and then halfway between each of those points, and so on. The outer edge may want to ruffle, but with gentle yet firm encouragement you will be able to make it lie flat.
5 Pin in place with T-Pins. My motto is "block the hell out of it" and it shall submit to your will.
6 Let dry.

STEAM BLOCKING

I am an advocate for wet blocking—I think it is the best way to block in almost every instance. If for some reason you are in a hurry and cannot wait for a piece to dry, you can try steam blocking. Because you don't want to iron your knitting directly, which could flatten and distort your stitches, you will need a piece of woven cloth that can withstand high temperatures, such as linen or cotton—no synthetic fibers. Be careful, steam can burn skin!

1 Dampen the cloth thoroughly and wring out excess moisture.
2 Carefully position your knitting on an ironing board, or a folded towel on the floor.
3 Place the damp cloth on the knit piece.
4 With a hot iron, carefully and quickly iron the cloth. You will be able to feel where your knits are.
5 Repeat until the knitting is nicely blocked, re-dampening the woven fabric if needed.

If you don't have a cloth, you can use just a steam iron, but hover just above the knitting (as shown in image above right). Press down occasionally and gently, always with the steam activated.

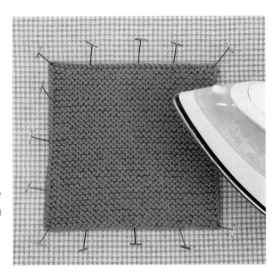

3D BLOCKING

3D knits such as hats might seem difficult to block, but I like to block hats on a balloon! I blow up the balloon to slightly smaller than I want the finished circumference of my hat to be, then balance it on a wide-mouthed jar. Place the washed hat over the balloon, making sure that the ribbing or edging is not stretched, and let it dry completely.

FINAL TOUCHES

Once you have knit, seamed, blocked, and dried your new knitting, you can add buttons, pom-poms and whatever else you fancy to finish it off.

SEWING BUTTONS

Sewing buttons on knitwear is done in the same way as sewing them onto fabric, with a few considerations. Remember that the thread and needle you use must fit through the button holes, so you'll likely have to use yarn thinner than you've knit with—I usually just use regular sewing thread and needle. You also want to make sure you catch entire pieces of yarn when you sew the buttons on, rather than piercing through the strands.

POM-POMS

I happen to like gadgets and enjoy using a pom-pom maker. But if you don't have one, never fear. You can create a pom-pom maker easily with just two circles of cardboard.

1 Cut two circles out of cardboard, slightly larger than you want your finished pom-pom to be.

2 In both, clip a small opening in the edge and cut a circle out of the middle. The hole in the middle should be slightly smaller than half the diameter of the outer circle. The bigger this middle hole, the less dense your pom-pom will be.

3 Place the cardboard circles together, with the openings lined up.

4 Wind the yarn around and around, wrapping as evenly as possible.

5 Keep wrapping until the center circle is nearly full.

6 With scissors, cut the outside edge of the wrapped yarn. Your scissors will be able to slide between the cardboard disks.

7 Tie a string around the cut yarn by sliding it between the disks.

8 Knot the string firmly, leaving long tails you can use for attaching the pom-pom.

9 Trim the pom-pom to a lovely spherical shape.

10 Attach the pom-pom to your piece with the long tails.

GLOSSARY

back (of work) the side of the work away from the knitter

binding off the closing stitches at the end of the work

casting on making stitches on the needle at the start of the work

chart a graph or grid with colors or symbols representing motifs or stitch patterns

Fair Isle a particular type of stranded color knitting, originating on the Shetland island of Fair Isle

front (of work) the side of the work facing the knitter

garter stitch a basic stitch pattern in which every stitch is knit

gauge the number of stitches and rows to a given measurement, also known as tension

knitwise inserting the needle into a stitch as if to knit

man-made yarns yarns from fibers made by chemical processes

natural fibers animal hair, such as alpaca, mohair, or wool; plant fiber, such as cotton or linen

purlwise inserting the needle into a stitch as if to purl

repeat a group of stitches or rows worked more than once to form a pattern

right side the side of the stitch pattern viewed when the item is complete

shaping using increases to make the fabric wider or decreases to make the fabric narrower

stockinette stitch a basic stitch pattern; knit on right-side rows, purl on wrong-side rows

wrong side the side of the stitch pattern that will not be seen when the item is complete

RESOURCES

YARNS

Berocco
www.berocco.com
Berroco, Inc.
1 Tupperware Dr. Suite 4,
N. Smithfield, RI 02896-6815
USA
401-769-1212

Cascade Yarns
www.cascadeyarns.com

Quince and Co
www.quinceandco.com

Wool and the Gang
www.woolandthegang.com
+44 (0) 207 241 6420

WEBSITES

www.craftsy.com
Try these Craftsy classes
- Modern Stranded Knitting Techniques, Mary Jane Mucklestone
- The Fair Isle Vest Stranded and Steeked, Mary Jane Mucklestone
- Knitting on the Bias, Bristol Ivy
- Save our Stitches, Laura Nelkin
- The Shetland Hap Shawl, Gudrun Johnston
- Magic Loop Knitting, Kate Gilbert

www.knitty.com
www.ravelry.com
www.twistcollective.com
www.maryjanemucklestone.com

BOOKS

150 Scandinavian Motifs: The Knitter's Directory, Mary Jane Mucklestone

200 Fair Isle Motifs: A Knitter's Directory, Mary Jane Mucklestone

Alice Starmore's Book of Fair Isle Knitting, Alice Starmore

Andean Folk Knitting: Traditions and Techniques from Peru and Bolivia, Cynthia Gravelle LeCount and Loren McIntyre

A Second Treasury of Knitting Patterns, Barbara Walker

A Treasury of Knitting Patterns, Barbara Walker

Color Knitting Techniques, Margaret Radcliffe

Designing Knitwear, Deborah Newton

Diagonal Knitting, Katharine Cobey

Domino Knitting, Vivian Hoxbro

Elizabeth Zimmermann's Knitting Workshop, Elizabeth Zimmerman

Fair Isle Style: 20 Fresh Designs for a Classic Technique, Mary Jane Mucklestone

Gossamer Webs: The History and Techniques of Orenburg Lace Shawls, Galina Khmeleva and Carol R. Noble

Heirloom Knitting, Sharon Miller

Japanese Inspired Knits, Marianne Isager

Knitted Tams, Mary Rowe

Knitter's Book of Finishing Techniques, Nancy Weisman

Knitting in the Nordic Tradition, Vibeke Lind and Annette Allen Jensen

Knitting in the Old Way, Pricilla A Gibson Roberts and Deborah Robson

Knitting with Two Colors, Meg Swansen and Amy Detjen

Knitting Nature, Norah Gaughan

Knitting Without Tears: Basic Techniques and Easy-to-Follow Directions for Garments to Fit All Sizes, Elizabeth Zimmerman

Little Red in the City, Ysolda Teague

The Knitting Workshop, Elizabeth Zimmerman

The New Encyclopedia of Knitting Techniques, Lesley Stanfield and Melody Griffiths

The Principals of Knitting, June Hemmons Hiatt

Vogue Knitting Ultimate Knitting Book, Editors of Vogue Knitting Magazine

INDEX

Page numbers in **bold** refer to illustrations

A

abbreviations, chart 115
afghan squares 45, 46, **46**, 47, **47**, 49, 68, 78, 94

B

backward loop cast-on 117, **117**
backward loop increases 121
bag, color field **13**, 68, **68**, **69**, 72–5, **73**, **74**
balanced single decreases 123
bar increase 97
beanie, chunky stockinette striped **28**, **30**, 33–5, 139
bias knitting 12, 15
  garter stitch triangles 44–51
  knitting chevrons 94
  mitered squares 60–7
binding off 42–3, 128–9
bird's eye pattern 39, **39**
blocking 136–7, **136**, **137**
buttons 138

C

capelet, triangle **12**, 56–9, **127**
casting on 116–17
charts 38–9, 86–7, 89, 115
chevrons 15, 15, 38, 39, 92–9
  chevron leg warmers **92**, 94, **94**, 97–9
circles 14, 14, 77
  daisy mat garter stitch circles 78, **78**, 79, **79**
  garter stitch and stockinette circles 76–83
  imperfect circles 87
  stranded colorwork dots 84–91
circular knitting 31, 37, 38, 43, 55, 58, 115, 124–5, 137
color: choosing 110–13
  customization 59
  and dots 85
  effect of on proportion 70
  and garter stitch 21
  joining new colors 51, 98
  and mitered squares 61, 63
  and stripes 29
  swapping out color 113
  and triangles 54, 55
  weaving in ends 133, 133
  working with two colors 119
color field bag **13**, 68, **68**, 72–5
colorwork, stranded 12, 14, 15, 126–7
  diagonal stripes 36–43
  dots 84–91
  triangles 52–9
corrugated ribbing 39, **39**
cowl, garter ridge möbius **20**, **21**, 25–6
crown shaping 35

D

daisy mat garter stitch circles 78, **78**, 79, **79**
decreases 46–9, 68–9, 93, 94, 98, 122–3, **122**
  balanced single decreases 123, **123**
diagonal stripes 11, 36–43
dishcloth, granny's 46, 49, **49**
domino knitting see mitered squares
dots: dotted mitts 84, **86**, 88–91
  stranded colorwork dots 84–91

E

edges: curling 30, 31
  zigzag 94
ends, weaving in 133

F

Fair Isle knitting 38, 55, 68–9, 86
  see also stranded colorwork
finishing techniques 130–9
floats 86, 93, 126

G

garter stitch 11, 15, 28, 30, 61, 94, 119, **119**
  garter stitch circles 76–83
  garter stitch stripes 20–7
  garter stitch triangles 44–51
  seaming 132–3, **132**, **133**
  weaving in ends 133, **133**
gauge 34, 41, 107
  measuring 114, **114**

H

haps 46
hats 137

chunky stockinette striped beanie **28**, **30**, 33–5, 139
multi-shape hat 101

I

increases 46–9, 93, 97, 98, 120–1, **120**, **121**
  backward loop increases 121
  lifted increases 120–1, **120**, **121**
  yarn over increase 121, **121**
intarsia 36

J

joins, nearly invisible 51

K

knit cast-on 116, **116**
knit stitch 118, **118**
  basic knit bind-off 128, **128**
knitting belt 127
knitting in the round see circular knitting

L

leaning increases 97
leg warmers, chevron **92**, **94**, 94, 97–9
lifted increases 120–1, **120**, **121**
long-tail cast-on 117, **117**

M

maakin' belt 127
magic loop technique 125
mattress stitch 132, **132**
mistakes, undoing 134, **134**
mitered squares 60–7, 68
  mitered square pillow **60**, **61**, **62**, 64–7, **102**
mitts, dotted 84, **86**, 88–91

möbius cowl, garter ridge **20**, **21**, 25–6
moss stitch 30

N
needles 104, **104**
  circular 50, 66, **104**, 124, **124**
  double-pointed 90, **104**, 124, 125, **125**, 127
  sizes 34, 82, 104, 105
  tapestry 105, **105**

P
pattern motifs 115
pennants 48, **48**, 49
pillow, mitered square **60**, **61**, **62**, 64–7, **102**
plain knitting *see* stockinette stitch
pom-pom makers 105, **105**, 138
princess line shaping 122
proportion 70–1
purl stitch 118, **118**
  purl bind-off 128, **128**

R
raglan shaping 71
rectangles 60
rib stitch 30–1, 119, **119**
  bind-off in rib 129, **129**
  corrugated ribbing 39
  ribbing bands 41–2
  weaving in ends 133, **133**
rows, ripping out 134, **134**
rugs, super chunky
  stockinette stitch circle **76**, **77**, 80–3, 137

S
scale 70–1
scarf, triangle stripe 101, **101**
seaming 30, 132–3
seed stitch 30, 119, **119**
selvedges 30
shades 113
shapes, mixing up 100–1
shaping 71, 120–3
shawls 12, 14, 44, 77
  haps 46
  triangular garter stitch shawl 44, 50–1
slipknot 116, **116**
spit-splicing 135, **135**
squares 13, 45, 69, 100
  mitered squares 60–7, 68
  proportion and scale 70–1
  stockinette stitch squares 68–75
steam blocking 137, **137**
steeking 55
stitches: basic stitches 118–19
  binding off 128–9, **128**, **129**
  casting on 116–17, **116**, **117**
  undoing stitches 134, **134**
  see also individual stitches
stockinette stitch 11, 15, 119, **119**
  seaming 132–3, **132–3**
  stockinette stitch circles 76–83
  stockinette stitch squares 68–75
  stockinette stitch stripes 28–35
storing knitwear 136
stranded colorwork 12, 14, 15, 126–7

diagonal colorwork stripes 36–43
  pattern motifs 115
  stranded colorwork dots 84–91
  stranded colorwork triangles 52–9
stripes 11
  diagonal colorwork stripes 36–43
  garter stitch stripes 20–7
  irregular stripe chevrons 95
  knitting neat stripes 31
  in ribbing 31
  stockinette stitch stripes 28–35
  triangle stripe scarf 101, **101**
swatches 107, 114
  daisy mat garter stitch circles 78, **78**, 79, **79**
  garter stitch stripes 22–4
  irregular stripe chevrons 95
  practising increases and decreases 46–9
  stockinette stitch 30, 32
  variegated yarn chevrons 96, **96**

T
tablet case, diagonal striped **11**, **36**, 39, 40–3, **138**, **140**
tails, leaving 133
3D blocking 137
three-needle bind-off 129, **129**
tints 113
tones 113
tools 104–5
triangles 12, 13
  garter stitch triangles 44–51

stranded colorwork triangles 52–9
triangle stripe scarf 101, **101**
troubleshooting 134–5

U
undoing stitches 134, **134**

W
waves 92
wet blocking 136, **136**

Y
yarn: ball bands 107, **107**
  carrying yarn 26
  choosing yarn 106–7
  holding the yarn 108, 126
  joining new yarns 98, 127
  and knitting chevrons 94
  knitting with double yarn 74
  nearly invisible joins 51
  spit-splicing 135, **135**
  stranded colorwork 126
  types of yarn 106
  value 113
  variegated yarn chevrons 96, **96**
  yarn dominance 126
  yarn substitution 106–7
  yarn weights 107
yarn over increase 121, **121**
yokes 71

Z
zigzags 15, 38, 39, 92, 93, 94
  zigzag edges 94

CREDITS

Thanks to all my students from all over the world—I learn so much from you.

Special thanks to Lucy Kingett who talked me down off the ledge many a time.

Thanks to the designers who were so kind to allow me to feature their inspiring work. Find below details of where you can find each of the featured patterns:

Amy Lawrence
amylawrencedesigns.co.uk; Etsy shop amylawrencedesigns
Knitted Chevron Necklace (page 15)
Knitted Thistle Necklace (page 93, left)

Carina Spencer
carinaspencer.com; Ravelry at CarinaSpencer
Western Auto Cowl (page 12, right)

Carrie Bostick Hoge
maddermade.com; Ravelry at Madder
Lila Raglan Sweater (page 71)

Elizabeth Brassard
coloriee.canalblog.com; Ravelry at Coloriee
Rainbow Magicowl (page 21, right)

Erin Black
midknits.com; Ravelry at midknits
Chevron Pumpkins (page 15, lower right)
Color Blocked Nesting Bowls (page 29, left)
Convertible Triangle Color Blocked Bowl (page 53, right)

Grace Akhrem
graceakhrem.com; Ravelry at Grace Akhrem
Random Stripes (page 11, left)
Olana Slouch (page 21, left)

Hilary Smith Callis
theyarniad.com; Ravelry at Hilary Smith Callis
Turntable (page 11, right)
Shadow & Glow (page 45, right)
Dots Cowl (page 85, left)

Jane Slicer-Smith
sigknit.com; Ravelry at Jane Slicer-Smith
Mitre Shona Long Jacket (page 61, left)

Jared Flood
brooklyntweed.com; Ravelry at brooklyntweed
Turn a Square (page 69, right)

Joji Locatelli
jojiknits.blogspot; jojiknits.com; Ravelry at jojilocat
Spectrum (page 94)

Kay Gardiner and Ann Shayne
MasonDixonKnitting.com; Ravelry at Kay Gardiner and Ann Shayne
New Log Cabin Washcloths (page 61, right)

Kirsten Kapur
kirstenkapurdesigns.com; Ravelry at throughtheloops.
Fort Tryon Wrap (page 69, left)

Laura Chau
laurachau.com; Ravelry at laurachau
Delicious Socks (page 29, right)

Laura Nelkin
nelkindesigns.com; Ravelry at LauraNelkin
Magpie Shawl (page 45, left)

Mary Jane Mucklestone
maryjanemucklestone.com; Ravelry at MaryJane
Muckle Mitts (page 15, left; page 93, right)
Fishbones (page 37, right)
Flying Geese Cowl (page 53, left)
The Fair Isle Vest (page 55)

Lichen Mitts (page 85, right)
Stopover (page 100, above)
Modern Colorwork Cowl (page 100, below)

Miss Knit Nat
missknitnat.com; Etsy shop Miss Knit Nat
Monochrome Triangle Knitted Headband and Snood (page 12, left)

Purl Soho
purlsoho.com; Ravelry at purlsoho
New Log Cabin Washcloths (page 70)

Romi Hill
designsbyromi.com; Ravelry at Romi
Urania's Tam (page 77, left)

Sarah Elwick
sarahelwick.com; available through Not on the High Street
Amazing Maze Scarf (page 37, left)

Seven Gauge Studios
sevengaugestudios.com; available through Not on the High Street
Geo Knitted Cushion in Inferno Red and Seal and Wedge Knitted Cushion in Oatmeal and Inferno Red (page 5, mid right-hand column)
Lolli Knitted Scarf in Inferno Red and Seal (page 14, above)
Knitted Spot Cushion and Geo Cushion (page 101)

Sophie Home
sophiehome.com
Mono Cushion and Modig Throw (shown on pages 62 and 102)

Susan Barstein
sknitsb.com; Ravelry at maxlabradoodle
Moon Pie (page 77, right)

Tanis Gray
tanisknits.com; Ravelry at TanisKnits
Polarized Hat (page 39)

Quantum Books would like to thank the following for supplying images for inclusion in this book: Getty Images, Venturelli / Contributor, pages 4 and 13 Seven Gauge Studios / image by Studio Photography Carmel King, page 5 (mid right-hand column) Shutterstock.com, Kamenuka, page 48 (top)

For bringing the projects to life, thanks to photographer Simon Pask and our lovely models: Frankie Moore, Emily Slaughter at Simon How Agency, and Grace St Hill at PARTS agency.

Many thanks to the following for supplying wallpaper:
The Romo Group, Ilsa Wallcovering Mimosa
    Reference no: W376/01
    www.romo.com
Harlequin & Scion, Axis 110836 By Scion
    Stockist no: 0845 123 6805
    www.scion.uk.com

For the generous supply of yarn, thanks to Cascade Yarns and Wool and the Gang.

Thanks also to Rachel Atkinson, Lucy Kingett, and Luise Roberts for their editorial work and technical expertise.